STRATEGIES FOR NURTURING
CUSTOMERS IN A WORLD OF CHURN

D1483529

SUBSCRIPTION
MARKETING

Second Edition

Anne H. Janzer

Subscription Marketing:
Strategies for Nurturing Customers in a World of Churn
Second Edition
Copyright © 2017 Anne H. Janzer

Cuesta Park Consulting

Mountain View, CA

Printed in the United States of America

ISBN: 978-0-9864062-5-6

Praise for
Subscription Marketing

"Keeping an existing customer is much more profitable than selling a new one, especially in a subscription business. Anne Janzer shows you how to add value and nurture customers before and after the sale, driving success in today's real-time business environment."

David Meerman Scott
Best-selling author of *The New Rules of Marketing and PR*, now in 25 languages from Arabic to Vietnamese

"Anne's terrific book is an excellent primer to help your business take advantage of the subscription economy, while navigating around potential potholes. And as a bonus: It's clear, straightforward, and refreshingly jargon-free!"

Ann Handley
Chief Content Officer, MarketingProfs, and author of the WSJ best seller, *Everybody Writes*

"Finally, a roadmap. Anne Janzer not only illustrates the power of truly understanding what drives value throughout the subscription customer lifecycle, but essentially gives us the very roadmap needed to make it happen."

Michelle Lange
Cofounder, SUBTA
(Subscription Trade Association)

"Although there is no 'holy grail' measurement for content marketing, there is one that sits atop the rest—the subscriber. As more organizations move from paid to owned media, acquiring and keeping subscribers to our information is more important than ever. Read Anne's book and you'll have everything you need to create and execute a subscription strategy that works."

Joe Pulizzi
Founder, Content Marketing Institute
Author of two best-selling books:
Content Inc. and *Epic Content Marketing*

"We all want customers to stay longer, buy more along the way, expand their relationship with us, and tell their friends and peers about us. And the only reliable way to consistently get those incredibly valuable results is to ensure our customers are continually getting more and more value from their relationship with us. Luckily, Anne's book shows you exactly how to do this."

Lincoln Murphy
Author of *Customer Success*,
Founder of Sixteen Ventures

"Anne Janzer has noticed what many marketers have overlooked: There's a 'silent revolution' taking place as more products and services are being sold on a subscription basis. With the publication of the second edition of *Subscription Marketing*, Anne Janzer goes deeper into the topic with fresh insights, examples, and suggestions for profiting from this proven strategy."

Roger C. Parker
Content Marketing Institute
Top-Ranked Blogger 2016

"Customer success teams need account-based marketing strategies to operate at scale. This book will teach you how to develop effective customer campaigns after the sale to increase adoption and growth."

Irit Eizips
Founder, CSM Practice

"Over the past five years, every marketing organization has been turned on its head. Author Anne Janzer does an outstanding job of detailing the new realities of value-based marketing in a subscription-dominated world. A must-read for every marketing organization, *Subscription Marketing* reveals the secrets and strategies for engaging and keeping customers for life."

Randy Brasche
Vice President of Marketing at Zignal Labs

"Selling into an installed base should be a core component of any Sales/Marketing strategy. And yet it's often overlooked. Janzer's excellent book focuses on this low-hanging fruit and how to leverage it for greater profitability. This book is required reading for anyone trying to maximize their marketing budget—which is everyone."

Tom Hogan
Founder and Principal, Crowded Ocean, coauthor of
The Ultimate Start-Up Guide

"Filled with great examples across industries, this book is a well-written and easy 'must-read' on why and how to add value for both subscriptions and non-subscription-based services alike."

Kathy Klotz-Guest
Founder, Keeping it Human, Inc.
Author of *Stop Boring Me!*

"In today's marketing organizations, customer success and customer engagement have never been more important. Creating compelling marketing programs for the new subscription economy is an exciting opportunity for teams willing to learn and take on the challenge."

John Robb
Entrepreneur, former VMware General Manager

Contents

Introduction   1

The Subscription Shift   13

Chapter 1 The Growing Subscription Economy   15

Chapter 2 Shifting to Subscriptions   27

Chapter 3 The Marketing Impact   39

Chapter 4 Rethinking the Funnel   47

Chapter 5 Value Nurturing   53

Value-Nurturing Strategies   61

Chapter 6 Create a Customer Launch Plan   63

Chapter 7 Orchestrate Early Success   69

Chapter 8 Help Customers Create New Habits   75

Chapter 9 Offer Great Training   79

Chapter 10 Share Customer Stories   81

Chapter 11 Quantify Your Value   85

Chapter 12 Celebrate Successes   89

Chapter 13 Create Value Through Content   93

Chapter 14 Create Community   101

Chapter 15 Nurture Your Fans and Advocates   107

Chapter 16 Ask for Advice and Input   115

Chapter 17 Handle Breakups Gracefully   119

Chapter 18 Share Your Story   123

Chapter 19 Embed Values in Your Business Model   131

Chapter 20 Nurture Free Trial Users   135

Putting the Strategies into Action   **143**

Chapter 21 The Business Case for Value Nurturing   145

Chapter 22 Start Nurturing Value   155

Chapter 23 Build Organizational Support   163

Chapter 24 Common Challenges and Risks   175

Chapter 25 Four Fundamental Rules of Value Nurturing189

Chapter 26 The Marketing Opportunity   197

Acknowledgments   201

Resources and Notes   205

About the Author   211

Index   213

Introduction

I've noticed a subtle change in my purchasing behavior in recent years: I buy less "stuff" than I used to. That's not because I've gone on a radical decluttering binge. No, it's because buying isn't my only option now. I can subscribe to things I would have previously purchased.

I don't buy as many CDs as I used to, although I listen to plenty of music. Instead of purchasing DVDs, I rent films from Netflix or Redbox, or stream them from Netflix and Amazon.

My office no longer features cabinets stuffed with software boxes and manuals. I subscribe to nearly everything, from my website and email platform to writing software and Microsoft Office 365. My broadband data and mobile phone plans (also subscriptions) make those digital services possible. Then there are things I've almost always subscribed to: my membership at the local YMCA, the *New York Times*—you get the idea.

Subscribing is an option for many of the daily choices in my life, and I suspect that is true for you as well.

How many passwords do you manage? That's one clue to your immersion in the ever-growing world of subscriptions. (If you're wise, you may also subscribe to a password manager to deal with this unwanted side effect.)

Generational issues also come into play. My adult children subscribe to many more services than I do, including ready-to-cook meals, clothing, razor blades, and who knows what else.

We are becoming a society of subscribers. Subscriptions ease the pain of making decisions. They alleviate the burdens of ownership and maintenance. They offer the convenience of automation or regular service. And, in the case of subscription boxes, they can be fun. Increasingly, we are clicking the Sign Up button or Subscribe button rather than the one labeled Buy Now.

What's Changed Since the First Edition

When the first edition of this book was published in January 2015, I encountered many quizzical looks. Subscription marketing? Is this book about selling magazines and newspapers?

That doesn't happen so much anymore.

Every month, more businesses commit to a recurring revenue model, or add a paid or unpaid subscription to their offerings. These include:

- Services to which people actively subscribe
- Cloud-based software with pay-as-you-go pricing

- Fee-based membership communities or purchasing programs
- Regularly scheduled, recurring purchases of physical or digital goods
- Professional or industrial services, including "managed services" packaging physical goods like printers or chemicals with supporting services.

To get a handle on the scope of this change, take a look at the Subscription Economy® Index developed by Zuora. Zuora makes subscription management software and champions the concept of the Subscription Economy. Zuora's customers are businesses that depend heavily on subscriptions, giving the company unique insight into what's happening with this trend.

Nearly every industry now participates in this growing sector of the economy. Start-ups launch with subscription models, while giant, established businesses are finding their way in. For example, Unilever paid a billion dollars to acquire a subscription razor blade company in 2016. If your own business isn't part of this Subscription Economy, your competitors probably are.

Pretty soon, we may have to simply call it *the economy*.

Zuora's Chief Data Scientist compiled aggregated data from its customer portfolio to create the Subscription Economy Index to reflect this cross-section of businesses. Looking at the period from January 2012 to September 2016, we see that sales for the Subscription Economy Index grew *nine times faster* than sales of the S&P 500, and four times faster than U.S. retail sales overall. The Subscription Economy is here, and it's thriving.

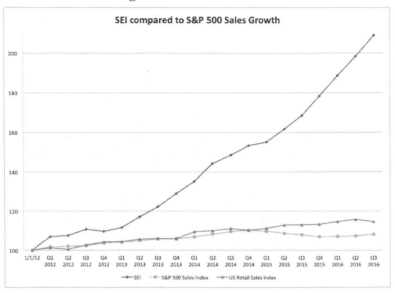

Sales growth for the Zuora Subscription Economy Index

Since the start of 2015, when the first edition of this book came out, subscription sales growth has been particularly steep. The practices in this book are relevant to many more businesses today than they were just two years ago.

A World of Churn

As subscription sales grow, so does the biggest challenge to growth: churn. Churn is what happens when customers leave or recurring revenues vanish. It is the opposite of growth.

We may subscribe to services because they are convenient, fun, or affordable. But there are just as many reasons to cancel or cut back subscriptions. We are quite happy to click

Unsubscribe. Again, a quick glance into your personal life illustrates the magnitude of the issue.

Do you ever sign up for a free trial of software that looks interesting, only to forget to use it? (I'm guilty of this one.)

Do you subscribe to online content, then months later, overwhelmed by all the messages in your inbox, go on an unsubscribing binge?

Do you periodically look for ways to dial down recurring subscription costs? For example, you might cut back on the number of devices on your cell phone plan, or the number of channels on a cable plan. Even though you remain a customer, this behavior represents *revenue churn*, or the loss of recurring revenue.

Do you swap out expensive subscription options for entirely different services, such as "cutting the cord" on cable and subscribing instead to multiple streaming services?

The barriers to churn are low. If you're using one subscription food delivery service and a friend tells you about a better one, you can switch in an instant. In the enterprise IT world, switching software subscriptions may entail training and transferring data, but it's still easier than deploying new application infrastructure.

We are subscribers inhabiting a world of churn.

The Zuora Subscription Economy Index contains sobering data about churn. The average annualized churn rate was 24 percent for business-to-business companies, and 31 percent in the business-to-consumer sector.

Do those numbers sound high? They are. As long as you're growing rapidly, you can survive. But if your business has that kind of churn rate, you can do something about it.

What This Means for Marketing

We live in a world of churn, but we do not have to accept high churn rates as the only reality.

In traditional business models, marketing and sales organizations worry about losing *new* sales to competitors. In a subscription business, your *current* customers are fair game for competitors. Because subscribers pay as they go, they decide repeatedly to remain a customer (renew) or leave for a competitor (churn). With no up-front capital investment in your business, they may be tempted to switch.

> In the Subscription Economy, you're only doing half of your job as a marketer if you focus on the sale and ignore the customer.

A relentless focus on churn (or, if you're an optimist, its counterpart: *retention*) is the duty of every marketer in a business with subscriptions.

High churn numbers represent an opportunity. If you can reduce churn rates through marketing campaigns or customers success efforts, you can have a significant and lasting effect on revenues and growth.

Churn may be indicative of all kinds of problems, many outside your control. Often, however, it results from a misalignment of the customer's expectations at sign-up and experience thereafter. The experience didn't pan out as the subscriber thought it would.

Subscription marketers can reduce churn numbers by:

- Understanding and addressing real-world customer needs
- Attracting the right customers, or those who will realize the most value from your solution
- Continuing to nurture the customer's experience of value long after the sale
- Forming long-lasting customer relationships that inspire loyalty and advocacy in the subscriber base

Traditional marketing strategies and techniques focus on leading people to the initial sale, turning prospects into customers. Subscription businesses shift their focus from the point of sale to the long-term, ongoing customer relationship. In effect, the subscriber remains a prospect, deserving ongoing engagement and nurturing.

This book suggests that marketers add a core objective to their practices: *value nurturing*. Value nurturing happens after the initial sale. Its objective is to help the customer achieve and realize value from the solution.

Value nurturing serves your long-term business interests. Customers who realize value are likely to renew their subscriptions; competitors must work much harder to lure them away. These customers may also purchase more from your business, whether by upgrading or buying other services. The most loyal customers refer others to your business.

Who Should Read This Book

In the first edition of this book, I tried to focus on the practices and skills of marketing professionals. In talking with people since that time, I've become convinced of the following truth:

> Organizational boundaries are the enemies of the subscriber experience.

The value-nurturing practices described on the following pages often happen outside the marketing organization. Many customer success teams include individuals tasked with creating and executing campaigns to bring new subscribers on board or to encourage feature adoption and renewal. They are effectively marketing after the sale.

In a successful subscription-based business:

- Marketers pay attention to what goes on throughout the entire customer journey, venturing out of comfortable organizational boundaries and silos.

- People in other parts of the organization adopt marketing practices and messaging.

This revised and expanded edition includes guidance and strategies that fall beyond the traditional domain of marketing, including subscription business model variations, cautionary tales about risks and challenges, and suggestions for organizational realignment to adjust to this shifting subscription-based world.

The strategies and concepts here are designed for:

- Any marketer in a business that currently has, or is considering, a subscription-based offering

- Executives in businesses making a transition to a subscription model, who need to understand the implications for both marketing strategies and overall cultural shifts

- Customer success teams looking for "low-touch" or automated strategies for promoting adoption and loyalty across thousands or tens of thousands of subscribers
- Executives managing mature subscription businesses and looking for ways to minimize churn while remaining relevant and valuable to subscribers
- Start-ups trying to "growth hack" their way to success

The examples included span business to-business (B2B) and business-to-consumer (B2C) companies in diverse industries. In the subscription context, Fortune 100 corporations and scrappy start-ups may have more in common than you might realize. Rather than looking at what your competitors are doing today, I encourage you to cast a wider net as you consider your own business and its customers.

Part One describes what's happening in the subscription shift across industries and how those changes affect marketing. It examines a variety of subscription business models, as well as the limitations of the traditional marketing funnel analogy. This section defines the practice of *value nurturing*—helping your customers realize value from the experience of being a customer.

Part Two includes a wide variety of value-nurturing strategies, including facilitating customer success, demonstrating value, adding value outside the solution, and aligning with customer values. This part also includes a chapter about that first moment of value nurturing, the free trial conversion. While the strategies in Part Two are grounded in marketing practices, remember that in a subscription-based business, everyone's in marketing. Really.

Part Three offers suggestions for putting the strategies in Part Two into practice. Topics include building the business case for value nurturing, expanding your marketing efforts after the sale, and making the organizational adjustments necessary to support a broader cultural shift toward nurturing subscribers. Read the chapter on the challenges and risks of subscription marketing to avoid common problems.

If you're just getting started with a subscription model, use this book to plan your course. If you're already underway with value nurturing, review the strategies in Part Two to expand your efforts. There's always room to improve and try new things.

We Can All Be Subscription Experts

As you read the chapters in this book, I'd encourage you to look at the world around you with a sense of curiosity. You experience subscription marketing tactics every day. Which ones resonate with you? How do they make you feel? What spurs you to take action?

We all have the potential to become creative and effective subscription marketers. The challenge is looking past the current accepted wisdom: how you've always done things, what your competitors do, and even what your industry does.

To be successful over time, businesses based on subscriptions maintain long-term customer relationships by adding, demonstrating, and nurturing value. You can look to almost any kind of business for inspiration.

You're already enrolled in a master class in subscription marketing. Look around you and learn.

Part One

The
Subscription
Shift

Chapter 1

The Growing Subscription Economy

Charles Dickens published his novels as serial installments in Victorian England. *The Pickwick Papers* issues were *The Sopranos* of the day.

The subscription business model has been around at least as long as the first magazines or newspapers. But new technologies have given it a boost, simplifying access to and distribution of goods and services, and making subscriptions possible in one industry after another.

We see these changes in our personal lives, as we sign up for subscription boxes, stream videos and music, and use web-based applications instead of buying packaged software. Subscriptions are reshaping the business landscape as well, changing how companies purchase everything from software to storage, telecommunications, printing, personnel services, supplies, chemicals, and more.

This shift to subscriptions isn't simply about revenues: It's really a story about human behavior.

Subscriptions work because we want them.

We subscribe to things for all kinds of reasons. It's more convenient to subscribe than to purchase. We have too many decisions in our lives, and subscribing reduces the decision-making load. Sometimes we join for reasons of identity and community. As Robbie Baxter says so eloquently in her book *The Membership Economy*, "membership provides recognition, stability, and convenience while connecting people to one another."

The growing trend of personalization also drives the subscription uptake. In a sea of automation and data, we want to feel recognized and acknowledged. To gather personalized insight, businesses must form long-term relationships with customers. They need you to subscribe.

The subscription or membership is the container for the long-term customer relationship. It's the battleground in the evolving information-driven economy.

> Subscription business models are changing our behavior.

We are becoming accustomed to businesses giving us what we want at the moment we require it, with instantly accessible, personalized services. The convenience and delight we experience in one area of our lives affects our expectations for other vendors. What started out as a way for companies to differentiate themselves is rapidly turning into a competitive requirement: table stakes for serving customers in the twenty-first century.

Because the subscription shift is behavioral as well as organizational, it's going to affect nearly every industry.

If you're not convinced, come with me on a quick survey of industries feeling the effects of the growing Subscription Economy.

Technology Shifts to the Cloud

For an object lesson in how subscriptions transform and disrupt industries, study the recent history of the software industry.

In the technology industry, software led the shift to subscriptions. Using software-as-a-service (SaaS), you don't have to buy packaged software, nor do you need to own the hardware to run your applications, or even manage and update them.

Salesforce pioneered the business-oriented SaaS market, giving companies of all sizes access to advanced Customer Relationship Management (CRM) software that previously was expensive and complex to implement. Today, Salesforce revenues exceed $6 billion a year.

As it turns out, most businesses and individuals would rather pay to access resources over the Internet, when they need them, than own them outright.

The technology industry "clouded up" very quickly. Analyst group Gartner tracks technology trends in its annual Hype Cycle reports, tracing trends from early, over-hyped expectations through disappointment to eventual mainstream adoption and acceptance.

In 2008, cloud computing was listed as more buzz than substance, in the "inflated expectations" part of the report. By 2011, cloud computing had its own Hype Cycle report. It went from an emerging technology to a *category of its own* in only three years. And it hasn't slowed down since.

Cloud computing has transcended the hype to transform the software industry, shifting market leadership and market share. As with many disruptive innovations, the existing players haven't gone away, but they've had to evolve or face significant competition from cloud-based entrants.

Established vendors are responding by launching cloud-based solutions, acquiring cloud-based competitors, or transitioning packaged software to service-based offerings. Microsoft now offers its popular Office products as cloud subscriptions (Office 365), while serving developers with its Azure Cloud Computing platform.

Research firm IDC suggests that in most software businesses, growth is happening in recurring, subscription-based sales rather than packaged software sales. According to IDC's Worldwide Software License, Maintenance, and Subscription Forecast, 2016–2020, subscription software revenues should reach $150 billion in 2017.

The writing is on the wall, at least for the software industry: For revenue growth, look to subscription-based offerings, not to traditional, "linear" sales models such as packaged software with perpetual licenses.

Subscriptions and Retail

If you want a master class in subscriptions and retail, look no further than Amazon.

When most of us think of Amazon, many of us picture its logo on boxes delivered to our doorsteps. We turn to Amazon for physical goods.

Amazon has used the power of the subscription model to fuel enormous retail sales growth with its Amazon Prime subscription.

Amazon Prime began as a subscription to free shipping, designed to lure returning shoppers. It comes at a cost—currently $99 per year. How does Amazon keep you coughing up the money for free shipping? By *adding value* to the subscription, through content, instant gratification, and convenience.

- *Valuable content*: Prime members can access free streaming videos, Kindle books, Audible channels, and music.
- *Instant gratification*: In addition to the two-day shipping that defines Prime, in some cases Prime members can get free *two-hour* shipping with Amazon Prime Now.
- *Convenience*: If getting off the couch and going to the computer is too much effort, use the Prime Now app on your phone. Get local restaurants to bring dinner to your door with Amazon Restaurants.

Beyond Amazon Prime, the company nudges you to create customized subscriptions to the goods you buy regularly. It offers discounts of up to 15 percent through its "Subscribe and Save" store.

The company is always looking for ways to anticipate customers' needs and meet them. Amazon has filed a patent for *anticipatory shipping*—shipping stuff before you actually order it. Keep an eye on what this giant retailer is doing.

Services Get In on the Subscription Act

Repeating services like gardening, pool maintenance, and cleaning are typically offered as subscriptions. When we bought our house, we subscribed to a termite inspection service that came out periodically.

For other professional services, we expect to pay as we need them, with hourly or one-time fees. Many of those providers, however, are finding ways to expand by offering online subscriptions to services. A quick web search uncovers a wide range:

- Physician house calls (NetMedNow)
- Legal advice (Rocket Lawyer)
- Therapy (Talkspace)
- Corporate recruitment services (Ascend HR Corp.)
- Financial planning (LearnVest)
- Accounting (Bench)

Industrial Goods as Subscription Services

Established vendors in business-to-business markets are adding value and building recurring revenue streams through *managed services* models. A managed service combines equipment and services as a subscription. The service provider retains ownership of any equipment, while managing and maintaining it on behalf of the customer.

Printer manufacturers like Xerox and HP offer managed print services to business clients, packaging the following services with the equipment:

- Working with the business customer to scope printing requirements (color, capacity, collation)
- Selecting the right building locations for the various printers
- Installing and configuring equipment
- Stocking paper and toner cartridges
- Maintaining the printers as necessary
- Reclaiming and replacing equipment as the business environment changes

How about industrial chemicals? Should businesses actually *own* the chemicals they use, or might they simply pay for the processes provided by that chemical? Using chemical leasing (or *chemical management services*), chemical manufacturers and distributors work with industrial customers to determine their objectives, then supply and manage the appropriate chemicals for the task at hand.

Suppliers are compensated for the *effectiveness* of their chemicals, not the volumes they sell. From an environmental perspective, everyone benefits by doing critical processes with fewer chemicals. The service providers have the necessary knowledge to handle and dispose of the chemicals safely and responsibly.

Want to try 3D printing without investing in the device yet? You can subscribe to an advance 3D printer from Carbon. In addition to the device, you'll get support services that help you test the possibilities of 3D printing in your business.

Subscription Boxes

In the consumer market, any goods or services that people use regularly are tempting candidates for subscription-based start-ups.

For variety and novelty, check out the growing trend in subscription boxes. Subscription box companies curate and ship collections of related goods, often in the hope that you will purchase follow-up versions of the items you like. The upsell is often part of the subscription.

A host of start-ups are testing subscription boxes for all kinds of goods, including:

Juice cleanse regimens

Food, meal-planning, and ready-to-prepare meals

Running gear

Cosmetics and beauty samples

Gaming gear

Toys

Ammunition

Pet food, supplies, and toys

3D printing supplies

Co-living spaces

Video courses

Hot sauce

Air travel

Chickens (oddly, there are several subscription chicken offers—you might say, even, a flock of them)

If subscription boxes are your thing, you can subscribe to Cratejoy to discover new boxes or build and manage your own box-based business.

Other Trends Accelerating the Shift to Subscriptions

If you need additional evidence about the inevitability of the coming growth in subscriptions, consider how they participate in other major trends.

The Sharing Economy: Sharing economy businesses are built on the concept that people really want *access* to goods, not *ownership* of them. The model works particularly well for things you only need occasionally. Sharing economy businesses often rely on subscriptions and memberships.

Consider the typical car-sharing service. You sign up or subscribe to a service. Then you reserve a car when you need it. Whether you're driving (Zipcar) or someone else is (Uber or Lyft), these services are rapidly becoming a viable alternative to owning a car. But the first step is subscribing.

Mobility: The mobile phone has become a powerful computing device, catering to our appetite for constant connectivity and instant gratification. Some pundits say that we are living in an On-Demand Economy. Mobile apps are key to many of today's start-ups, and many of those apps have a paid subscription component.

Internet of Things: The term *Internet of Things* (IoT) refers to the growing number of devices with embedded

Internet connectivity. Whether it's a watch nudging you to stand up, a thermostat tracking your presence, or a remote industrial site self-reporting an anomalous reading, the Internet of Things grows larger with each passing day.

In a world of networked appliances, consumers maintain ongoing relationships with the vendors through mobile or web-based applications. The Internet of Things opens up the possibility for vendors of devices to offer subscription-based services alongside the devices they sell.

Devices like smart thermostats (Nest), wearable fitness technologies (Fitbit and others), and solar panels all have their own apps. Today, IOT vendors make most or all of their revenues from the sale of the device itself rather than the accompanying app. But the existence of this data creates opportunities for businesses to offer subscriptions using data collected.

Fitbit, for example, provides its application and software for free when you purchase the device, but offers a premium subscription with extra reporting and analysis. This is one example of a *freemium* model, in which a majority of customers use a free service supported by the smaller number of customers who pay for premium capabilities.

Digitization: The digitization of consumer goods makes it easier to build subscription services around them. The music industry, for example, has seen shifts from physical media (CDs) to digital media (iTunes and MP3s) to streaming media services, in which you do not own the music at all. The move to online delivery made it possible to *subscribe* to music, either as a supplement to purchased CDs or instead of ownership.

Resource Scarcity: With more than seven billion people on the planet, there's no escaping the fact that we live in an age of increasing scarcity. As businesses adapt to a world of dwindling resources, they will start working with their customers to reduce waste or reclaim materials.

The term *circular economy* refers to a model in which resources are reused and refurbished rather than mined and tossed into landfills. Carpet tile manufacturer Interface pioneered the idea of carpeting-as-a-service to close the loop on carpet manufacturing and recycling. Interface offers customers the option of leasing carpeting for commercial buildings, then reclaims and recycles the tiles when they are no longer needed. This business model significantly reduces the environmental footprint of the carpeting.

The circular economy is only possible if the company providing the product retains ownership within the context of a sustained relationship with its customers. Often, that ongoing relationship is a subscription.

We Are All Participants in the Subscription Economy

If you think your industry cannot be disrupted by subscriptions, you're not thinking hard enough.

Tien Tzuo, CEO of Zuora and a vocal advocate of the Subscription Economy, makes this bold claim: "In five years, you won't buy anything, but subscribe to everything."

That may or may not be true, but here's my take: In five years, you'll have the *option* of subscribing to everything—and every business will have to accommodate that fact.

Chapter 2

Shifting to Subscriptions

Subscriptions will never replace all other business models, and the subscription trend is not emerging evenly across all industry segments and sectors. But if you look carefully, you can find it happening nearly everywhere.

Many established businesses are adding subscriptions to their offerings, while others have made the complete shift to this model, abandoning one-time sales altogether. Most start-ups use a subscription model from day one.

In this chapter, we will look at the various ways businesses are shifting to subscriptions. One size definitely does *not* fit all businesses. By considering a range of options, you may find the path that makes the most sense for your purposes. If your business is already subscription-based, you may find inspiration for expanding your offerings.

This chapter is not meant to be a guide to shifting business models. For an in-depth discussion of the move to subscriptions, consider reading Robbie Kellman Baxter's book *The Membership Economy*, and *The Automatic Customer* by John Warrillow.

Adding Subscriptions to an Existing Business

Established businesses have many options for joining the Subscription Economy. Some dive in head first, making the full transition to subscription sales. Others dip a toe into the water with a trial offering or a segment of the customer base. Common adoption models include:

- The subscription trial
- The segmented approach
- The "all-in" pivot
- Subscriptions as a marketing strategy
- Subscriptions as a start-up strategy

We'll take a quick tour through the advantages and challenges of each approach.

The Subscription Trial

Cautious companies may give the subscription model a trial run without making substantive changes to existing product and solution sales. Essentially, these businesses are saying, "Let's put out a subscription-based version of our traditional solution and see if anyone buys it."

While this seems like a relatively low-risk approach, the inherent lack of commitment may doom the trial to failure. In fear of cannibalizing current revenues, salespeople may not push the subscription. Marketing teams may not adequately research the ideal customer for this particular offering. Without investing in an onboarding process that guides subscribers to rapid success, businesses may experience high churn rates as customers fail to renew.

The financial results of a short trial may be underwhelming as well, since it takes time for subscription revenues to accumulate. Disappointing revenues from a subscription product confirm the skeptic's hypothesis that a subscription model doesn't fit the market. Failure becomes a self-fulfilling prophecy. You'll hear rationalizations like "*Our* buyers aren't interested in subscriptions" or "That doesn't work for what *we* do."

Complacency can be dangerous in competitive markets.

Give the subscription model a fair trial.

Allow enough time. When selling packaged goods or one-time services, all the revenue comes up front, at the point of the sale. Subscription revenues are earned *over time*. Revenues from a trial may look paltry at the start of the trial.

Commit resources. Spend the effort promoting not only the initial sign-up, but also the ongoing value of the subscription. If you don't take the extra steps to increase the value that customers realize after the sale, you're not likely to achieve success.

Experiment with the subscription offer. Do you take everything you offer and lump it as a subscription? Could you package one part of your total offerings, or create an entirely new combination that makes sense as a subscription? Develop a solution that aligns with your core value proposition and market needs.

If you take these steps, your subscription trial might just turn into an ongoing part of your solution offerings.

Serving a Segment with Subscriptions

Selling the same product with different pricing and delivery models presents challenges for your sales team. One solution is to segment the market you target with a subscription model, then dedicate marketing and customer success efforts to that segment. Using this approach, you can develop targeted value propositions for the distinct markets.

A few years back, I worked with a company that sold identity and access management software to large institutional clients. Those clients purchased, installed, and ran the software, with support from the vendor (my client). The company then developed a cloud-based offering to target the small and mid-sized business market. The subscription offering let them address a new market with software-as-a-service.

The company created a separate product line, branding, and website for the cloud-based version of its software, recognizing that the long-term business opportunity belonged in the cloud. The packaged software became a secondary offering that supported the launch of the subscription business. Segmenting the customer base was key to this company's subscription shift.

Using a subscription model can serve as a useful test case for a new market segment, if you do the research to understand the segment's needs.

Eventually, you may have to decide which model will get most of your development and marketing effort going forward. At that point, you might execute a *subscription pivot*.

The Subscription Pivot

In the software world, Adobe® Systems is the most visible example of a company pivoting from traditional to subscription models. Adobe started by shifting the sales model for its popular portfolio of design software, including Adobe Photoshop and Adobe Illustrator.

In October 2011, Adobe launched Creative Cloud® as a subscription, cloud-based version of its packaged design software. Adobe maintained both subscription and packaged versions of the software for more than a year.

In May 2013, the company announced that it would no longer update the packaged software, but would focus its development efforts exclusively on the cloud-based version. According to Adobe's press release announcing the shift on May 6, 2013, the decision was about accelerating innovation:

> Focusing development on Creative Cloud will not only accelerate the rate at which Adobe can innovate but also broaden the type of innovation the company can offer the creative community.

Adobe took heat from the press and investors at the time. Shifting revenues to a recurring model inevitably means a short-term revenue drop before long-term growth. But the company stayed on course, expanding its software-as-a-service commitment with Adobe Marketing Cloud and Document Cloud.

In late 2016, the company reported record revenues of $5.85 billion, with 78 percent of total revenues coming from subscriptions. Patience and a firm commitment paid off.

Subscriptions as a Marketing Strategy

In certain situations, the subscription model doesn't *threaten* existing business models—it supports and enhances them. Businesses add subscriptions for the purpose of driving revenues to existing, one-time offerings, or strengthening customer relationships and loyalty.

You probably receive offers to subscribe to things you purchase. My regular tea supplier, Adagio Teas, noticed that I frequently buy a particular variety of tea, and offered me the chance to subscribe to it.

Online retailers have discovered that adding a subscription can increase sales of products outside the subscription. It reduces the customer's "pain of paying" by lumping the decision to purchase many times into a single decision to subscribe. Plus, subscriptions are a real convenience for many customers.

A subscription can also function as a cross-sell offer to existing customers. Traditional retailers that add a curated monthly "box" subscription expose their customers to new products while strengthening the relationship.

For example, a growing number of companies offer subscriptions to monthly boxes of cosmetics and beauty supply samples. These businesses generate revenues not only from the subscriptions to the boxes, but also through further sales of the products in the box.

Or consider Amazon Prime, mentioned earlier, which is only *one* of the massive retailer's subscription offerings. For $99 per year, the Amazon Prime membership includes two-day shipping for eligible goods, free streaming of Prime Instant Video television and movie selections, Kindle book borrowing privileges, photo storage, and other benefits.

Although you pay to join Amazon Prime, the free two-day shipping has to cost Amazon real money. But Prime members tend to purchase more from Amazon. Consumer Intelligence Research Partners reports that Amazon Prime members in the U.S. spend on average $1,200 a year on Amazon, about twice the amount spent by nonmember Amazon customers. In its annual report, Amazon refers to Amazon Prime as an effective worldwide marketing tool.

Subscriptions as a Start-Up Strategy

What if you could launch a business with a strong base of customers already on hand? A growing number of start-ups use subscription content to find their initial customer base and build their first products.

In his book *Content Inc.,* Joe Pulizzi profiles a number of businesses that started with subscription content, engaging with and listening to the audience until they understood market needs. Only then did they roll out solutions, whether products or services.

The model worked well for Pulizzi's own start-up, the Content Marketing Institute, as well as numerous other businesses profiled in the book.

This is the opposite of running in "stealth mode" for months and then bursting upon the market, you hope, in a blaze of glory. Using the *Content Inc.* model, you start by interacting with potential customers in a meaningful way, delivering value through content while you learn from them.

If you're at the start of your business journey, consider building subscription relationships *first*, then figuring out what products best serve those relationships. A strong, positive audience can be a significant competitive advantage for your start-up.

> Other businesses might be able to copy your solution offering, but they cannot copy your customer relationships.

What Happens Behind the Scenes

A subscription model affects various parts of your business, including sales, finance, research and development, and customer success. Whether you are changing business models or adding subscriptions to your menu of offerings, you will have to answer difficult questions, such as:

- How do you sell subscriptions alongside another sales model?
- How do you compensate salespeople?
- Who handles renewals?
- Do you recognize revenues when the customer makes a commitment, or at the conclusion of the subscription time period?
- Is the solution messaging the same for all business models?

- Are you reaching a different part of the market with the subscription model? Are the customer personas the same?
- How do you price the subscription to support long-term business growth?

Making the transition to subscriptions can be difficult. Old ways of doing things don't work well. If you don't adjust to these differences, you may not experience the revenue growth you expect.

The subscription model may bring unexpected *benefits* beyond the obvious ones of predictable revenue streams and long-term customer relationships. These include:

Competitive differentiation: If you are the first in your market to offer subscriptions, the model can be a significant advantage. With a steady eye on subscriber usage and churn, you may be more attuned and responsive to market changes than competitors that sell once and walk away.

Market expansion: Subscriptions may open new market opportunities by making your solutions accessible and reducing the entry price point.

Other benefits: As a company Adobe struggled for many years with people using pirated copies of its software, particularly for costly Creative Cloud applications like Photoshop. The subscription model automatically reduces piracy, since the company no longer ships packaged software that can be copied. Further, organizations on tight budgets with single projects can pay to use the service for only a month or two.

For an example of the challenges and benefits of changing business models, let's follow one service business that made the switch.

A Case Study: Shifting an Established Business to Subscriptions

When you shift to a subscription model, you have the chance to ask fundamental questions about the way things are done. When Ascend HR Corporation, based in Houston, started offering recruiting services as a subscription, it ended up redefining the nature of the relationship between recruiting agency and client company for the better.

Most outsourced recruiting firms charge clients on a "per placement" basis. Companies hire the firms to find people for difficult-to-fill executive or technical positions, and pay a fee for each successful hire. Ascend HR Corp. decided to offer its services as a monthly or annual subscription.

With hindsight bias, it seems like a brilliant idea. But during the eighteen months or so of the transition to this model, the company had to solve many problems.

According to Rollis Fontenot III, Ascend HR Corp.'s president and business development director, determining the right pricing for the subscription model was a challenge. "We had no template, no starting point. We had to determine pricing levels and corresponding service offerings by trial and error. We've learned the need for simplification and clarification of our offerings as much as possible."

The sales cycle grew longer as well. With a traditional contingency fee model, clients do not pay until someone is hired, which could take months. With the subscription model, the customer pays a relatively small monthly fee at the beginning of each month. So Ascend HR must earn client trust in the relationship from the start.

After about a year and a half of transition, the company now operates almost exclusively on a subscription basis. Before making the change, revenues were variable. Now revenues are consistent, and the company has experienced an increase in annual revenues after the shift. Says Fontenot, "We have seen our revenues increase by 65 percent over the two years since making the transition. Our use of cloud-based technology helps us provide innovative solutions to clients while remaining cost-effective."

Expenses are now predictable for Ascend HR Corp.'s clients as well. Because fees could be large in the old model, hiring managers might delay signing a new employee to defer the expense to a later fiscal quarter. With the subscription model, it does not matter how many positions are filled or when the hire happens; the fee is the same. Clients can budget their recruitment costs accurately.

At one of its major clients, Ascend HR Corp. placed thirty-three people in three months. In the traditional per-hire pricing model, the client would have paid many times over the monthly fee in contingency fee costs.

However, the most important benefit of this shift is that it changes the nature of the relationship between Ascend HR and its clients, eliminating the inherent conflict built into the contingency pricing model.

The traditional fee-for-hire model often puts the hiring company and recruiting agency in conflict with each other. If the hiring company can fill a position, it avoids paying the recruiter's fee. In a sense, recruiters and their clients compete for the hire, which can inhibit information sharing. Recruiters don't have to disclose what they are doing to fill a position, since each party has an incentive to guard its own candidates.

With the subscription model, everyone is working toward the same objective: filling the empty positions. Recruiters and hiring managers share information freely.

The transition, although challenging, has turned out well for Ascend HR Corp. With recurring revenues lined up, the business environment feels less stressful and more rewarding, since the company fuels its own success by helping its clients grow.

Chapter 3

The Marketing Impact

Perhaps you are now convinced of the scope and breadth of the Subscription Economy, and of the many ways that businesses can use subscriptions.

This chapter brings these lessons home to the marketing organization. For example, what does it mean to you that your business's revenue model is changing? How is the role of marketing shifting and evolving in successful subscription businesses? Do subscriptions make marketing more or less relevant to the business?

Let's dive in.

Revenue Relevance

How relevant is marketing to your business?

It's a sensitive question. Most dedicated marketers feel that the work we do is important. Yet a surprisingly low number of marketing organizations track their effect on overall business performance and revenues.

Marketing's relevance depends, in great part, on its ability to affect ongoing revenues.

Historically, the role of marketing has been to attract customers or deliver prospects to a sales team, with the hope that those leads turn into revenue. Particularly in business-to-business or B2B companies, marketers have focused almost exclusively on generating leads, nurturing prospects, and enabling sales. For many years, that commitment has served businesses well.

But in a subscription business, revenue does not all arrive at the point of the sale.

Subscription offerings have lower up-front prices than packaged or one-time sales because customers pay as they go. Over time, if the subscriber remains a customer, the *lifetime value* of that relationship grows, even without cross-sell or upsell activities.

The longer you stay in business with a subscription model, the more of your revenues shift to a recurring model—*if* your customers stick around. Your success depends on customers staying. If you focus only on the moment of the sale, you're missing the bigger picture.

> To remain relevant as a subscription marketer, follow the revenues and focus on what happens after the moment of conversion.

Marketing organizations that remain focused exclusively on lead generation risk becoming less and less relevant to the business as a whole.

I am not suggesting that marketing's role is less vital in a subscription business. On the contrary, marketing plays a critical role, *if* it steps up to the realities of subscriptions.

Marketers who don't take action risk falling into the *marketing-revenue gap*. They spend their time and resources on one part of the revenue stream (net new revenues), while long-term business success depends on the current customer base (recurring revenues).

To avoid the gap, look past the traditional lead-generation and lead-nurturing activities, and even beyond the traditional scope of the marketing organization.

Understand the Math

As a savvy, revenue-relevant marketer, you should understand the financial payback of your marketing investment. To determine where to invest effort and resources for a subscription business, ask the following questions:

- What's the average cost of acquisition for a customer? How much does it cost to move a customer through the sales process, accounting for marketing and sales activities?
- What is the average revenue per account (ARPA)?
- What is the cost to serve that customer?
- Given the cost of serving the customer, how long does it take the subscription customer to repay the

cost of acquisition and become profitable? How many renewal cycles must pass?

- How long does the average customer remain and renew? What is the current churn rate?

When you account for the costs of acquisition and operations, a subscription customer is rarely profitable when they first sign up, even if they pay for a year up front. If you spend $100 to acquire a customer and the subscription fee is $5 per month, then a subscriber must remain a paying customer for twenty months to recoup acquisition costs alone. That time frame doesn't include the operational costs of serving the customer.

Scout Analytics (now part of ServiceSource) examined data on acquisition and operational costs from various sources and determined that the average break-even point for subscription software is 3.1 years. Your mileage may vary.

When first building a subscription practice, many companies focus exclusively on quickly adding customers. It's understandable. But the early days of a subscription are your best opportunity to establish practices for sustaining customer relationships in the future.

Consider aligning marketing spending and efforts with the *revenue opportunity* from existing customers, not just the revenue that customers are producing today. Calculate revenue potential based on how long you expect subscribers to remain and their potential for further sales. Chapter 21, *The Business Case for Value Nurturing*, discusses this topic in greater detail.

Churn is a critical metric to understand. How long do customers keep renewing? How many drop off each month or year? A high churn rate can indicate all kinds of problems, including design or delivery issues, or quality and usability glitches. But high churn often results from issues that marketing *can* address: You're attracting the wrong type of customer, or you're not doing enough once someone signs up.

> A successful subscription marketer maintains a relentless focus on customer churn.

The New Marketing Imperatives: Trust and Value

When you shift from one-time sales to subscriptions, the nature of the customer relationship itself changes.

A subscription is an ongoing relationship, not a one-time transaction.

This shift has implications for how you acquire customers initially and how you keep them happy over time.

In the traditional one-time-sale model, marketing does whatever it takes to influence the decision to purchase. Marketing practices focus on competitive differentiation, promoting the features and value of the solution, and making the emotional connections to spur the sale.

But customers signing up for a long-term relationship may require a different kind of convincing. They must *trust* in your company, not just the solution, to know that you'll be around. They need to feel that you won't try to rip them off or trap them in a relationship they cannot exit. And they must continue believing that they made the right decision in subscribing.

How does this shifting relationship change marketing responsibilities?

- Before the sale (the moment of subscription or conversion), marketing *demonstrates value* and *earns trust.*
- Once someone subscribes, marketing's role is to *nurture value* and *sustain trust.*

Marketing isn't the only group on the hook for these objectives. Marketing may set the tone and expectations, but the customer relationship exists between your customer and your entire company. Demonstrating value and sustaining trust requires cooperation between marketing, customer success, customer support, sales, service, and other groups.

> Marketing creates the promise. The whole business fulfills it.

Countless excellent books describe marketing before the sale. Here, we will consider what happens *after* the sale or initial subscription.

Focus Beyond the Conversion

When I worked at a start-up early in my career, we obsessed over lead generation. In desperate times, we'd resort to buying lists of leads from magazines or other sources—anything to keep feeding leads to the hungry sales team.

The VP of marketing characterized the relationship with sales this way: "We catch 'em, you skin 'em." I hated the analogy, but it represented the state of the world at the time quite well.

Today we live in a more enlightened marketing era. Marketing practitioners create useful content based on buyer personas. We add keywords to content so that it appears when prospects research online. We track, score, and nurture leads through the sales cycle with the assistance of marketing automation solutions.

But the fundamental pressure remains to generate leads worthy of handing off to sales. In most cases, the marketing investment stops with the acquisition of the customer. Some marketing organizations are evaluated and incentivized purely on the basis of lead generation or new customer acquisition.

These metrics are short-sighted when your business depends on recurring revenues.

> In the Subscription Economy, you're just getting started when someone becomes a customer.

Given the long-term revenue potential of customers in the subscription model, marketing must shift its focus past the point of the sale to the ongoing customer relationship. As David Meerman Scott writes in the wonderful *The New Rules of Sales and Service,*

> You keep customers happy by doing exactly the same things that won them in the first place. You win customers by focusing on their needs. You keep them the same way.

Chapter 4

Rethinking the Funnel

Avinash Kaushik, a digital marketing evangelist from Google, kicked off the MarketingProfs B2B Forum in October 2015 by announcing that the marketing funnel was dead. (Actually, he used a not-safe-for-work manifesto about the funnel, but you get the idea.)

All around me, I could hear the shuffling of speakers and presenters going through their presentations, searching out the slides with funnels and wondering if it was too late to make a last-minute change.

Every marketer has the image of the sales and marketing funnel implanted in their brains. It's a linear, one-way path that prospects travel to happiness and, one hopes, sales.

But as is often the case, the simple story line masks a much more complicated situation.

We have to get over our obsession with the funnel if we're going to change the way we think about customers after the sale.

Why the Funnel Metaphor Doesn't Work

You've seen it so many times: The marketing or sales funnel starts with a broad reach and then narrows to the eventual sale. Most marketing activities line up with that linear process. We speak of "top of funnel" activities and "feeding the funnel."

For marketers with a funnel mindset, the tasks of customer engagement start broad and quickly narrow down.

- **Brand recognition** activities have a wide reach and generate awareness, feeding the top of the funnel.
- Once a prospect is aware of your company, the next step is to **generate leads**, typically by collecting information in a registration form or at an event.
- As the prospect moves closer to a decision, marketing organizations deliver content for **lead nurturing** and sales enablement to move the prospect through the sales cycle to the purchase.

There are serious problems with the funnel metaphor:

- It treats the sales process like an inevitable, linear path, when reality is rarely so simple.
- It generally disregards whatever happens after the sale.

Ultimately, the staying power of the funnel metaphor imperils marketing's ongoing relationship with the customer. Because the current customers are beyond the critical part of the funnel, they seem less relevant to marketers.

Sure, we recognize the importance of engaging with customers. We reach out to them for success stories and testimonials, and brag about the more impressive ones. We hold user conferences and give their names to the press. But our processes and priorities are skewed toward brand recognition and lead generation.

How Subscriptions Kill the Funnel

What happens when you switch to a subscription sales and marketing organization? The subscriber continues to contribute revenue after the initial sign-up. Marketers who want to remain relevant continue nurturing the customer after the sale.

> The subscription model is the nail in the coffin of the simplistic, one-way funnel.

In a subscription business, marketing's impact on revenue doesn't end at the point of sale.

If you accept that existing customers are critical to subscription revenue and business growth, then you also must accept that the initial sale is *not* the endpoint in a subscription business. It's just a beginning.

You cannot abandon lead generation or nurturing efforts. But marketing's work is not done once the sale is made. The funnel metaphor ignores the other feedback loops built into the subscription marketing process, such as:

- Nurturing existing customers so that they renew
- Upselling existing subscribers
- Soliciting customer referrals, which then feed back into new lead generations

In the subscription model, the sales process has significant feedback loops. It's no longer a linear, one-way path. If you start drawing all these loops onto the traditional funnel image, you end up with something that looks more like a French horn than a funnel. And everyone knows that the French horn is difficult to master.

How About a Journey Instead?

The *customer journey* may be a better metaphor than the funnel. It is the path that the customer takes in interacting with your company and solution.

The journey metaphor puts the customer's *experience* at the center of attention, not their status with your company.

Considered from this perspective, a person travels from being unaware of your business (or their business problem) to considering your solution. At some point, they may move from consideration to purchase, but perhaps not for a while. Some prospects will take a winding, convoluted path to a purchase. Along the way, prospects may need specific content and resources to solve their problems.

To successfully engage with the customer journey, marketing organizations must understand how their solutions fit in customers' lives, from where they look for answers to problems to how they buy and use things. This insight derives from customer research and a strong sense of the problems to be solved.

The customer's journey doesn't end with the purchase. Subscribers start using the solution. It meets their requirements or doesn't. Then they face fresh challenges, or things change. In a B2B context, the customer's business may grow or shift. Life goes on after the purchase.

Whether or not your business remains part of that ongoing story depends, in part, on what you do after the sale.

The demise of the funnel brings opportunities to tell stories and engage with customers, and to forge an expanded role for marketing. Subscription marketers should add processes and campaigns that support the ongoing customer journey. These processes have many labels, including customer advocacy, retention, upselling, etc. We'll group all these activities under the broader term of customer value nurturing, or more simply, *value nurturing*.

Find the *Right* Customers

A subscription is a two-way relationship, and not all customers are created equal. In a traditional, one-time sales model, it didn't really matter if you sold a product to someone who wasn't a great fit. They might return it, but usually they didn't.

In a subscription model, it *does* matter if subscribers stick around. Remember that it can take several renewal cycles for a customer to pay back the costs of acquisition and service.

Rather than focusing on *how many* leads you generate, consider how to attract the prospects who will find success with the solution and remain loyal customers. This may mean forgoing the thrill of the lead-generation "hit" and focusing instead on generating fewer, highly targeted prospects.

To find the best-converting customers who stick around, pay attention to the behaviors of your most successful customers. Then, figure out how to change your marketing practices to attract more people like them.

- Identify target customer segments and personas who are a good fit.
- Identify the stages in the customer journey for those personas.
- Provide content and support at each phase of the journey, from initial awareness to the customer's long-term success.

In this model, marketing and customer success become one seamless part of the customer's journey.

Chapter 5

Value Nurturing

Beginning golfers are taught to work on their *entire* swing, including the follow-through. The follow-through on a golf swing affects where the ball goes once you hit it.

Value nurturing is like the follow-through for marketing and sales, ensuring that customers continue on the course you want them to travel.

Before the initial sale, you find prospects through thought leadership and lead generation. Lead-nurturing activities convince prospects of the potential value they can get from your solution. If you are successful, the prospect becomes a customer. *Value nurturing* is the marketing follow-through for that activity.

> Value nurturing is the act of supporting the customer's experience of value.

Once the sale is complete, other parts of the organization come into play, but marketing still has a significant role. Marketing can set customers on the path to achieving the functional or financial results they expected from signing up.

Marketing can gently nudge customers to *recognize* the fact that they are being successful. And, creative marketers add value *outside* the solution, through content, community, additional services, or the quality of the relationship experienced by the customer.

Value nurturing turns customers into loyal or repeat customers, and successful customers into advocates.

There's nothing revolutionary about the idea of marketing to current customers. You might feel that I'm stating the obvious here. But looking at the practices of many businesses around me, I often feel that customers are neglected. I've heard of large organizations that treat "customer marketing" as a backwater, *not* where the creative and visible campaigns happen. This mindset has to change.

Subscription customers deserve renewed marketing attention. For that reason, I suggest creating new label—*value nurturing*—that identifies the process as being of equal importance to lead generation and lead nurturing.

Many business activities can fall under the value-nurturing umbrella:

- **Customer success management:** Today this term is associated with a function that lives either in support or sales, rarely in marketing. Yet to scale up customer success efforts across tens of thousands of customers, you have to deploy marketing campaigns. Value nurturing is customer success executed at scale.

- **Customer retention:** Most customer retention efforts focus on finding customers at risk of leaving and convincing them to stay. The term typically applies to solving problems rather than creating value.

- **Upselling and cross-selling**: These are important results of successful value nurturing, but never mistake *selling* for creating value.

Value nurturing as defined here is a specific set of activities that take place after lead generation, lead nurturing, and customer conversion. It is the next logical step in subscription marketing.

The word *value* has inherent ambiguity that is useful in this particular case. Consider common uses of the word:

1. Value (*verb*): to consider something or someone as important or useful (Shakespeare: "I was too young that time to value her, but now I know her.")

2. Value (*noun*): a relative assessment of worth or importance ("What's the value of this painting?")

3. Value (*noun*): a principle or standard of behavior (Gandhi: "Your habits become your values, your values become your destiny.")

Value nurturing can confirm the customer belief that the ongoing subscription is a smart economic decision. Marketing can also increase the customer's perception of the relative value of a solution over time. These activities reinforce the first two definitions of value.

Last but not least, marketing may also align the solution with the customer's personal values (definition #3). Many people are interested in doing business with organizations that share their core values. This fact is spurring a growth in purpose-driven marketing related to social or environmental issues.

This third type of value, the alignment of principles or ideals, carries particular weight in the Subscription Economy because the customer maintains an ongoing relationship with the vendor.

Whose Value Is It, Anyway?

It's tempting to align value nurturing with monetary metrics such as *customer lifetime value*. How much money does the customer contribute to the business over the course of their relationship? How can you optimize that?

Revenue growth is, of course, your endgame. But if you approach value nurturing purely with the thought of getting more money from existing customers, you're likely to get it wrong. We've all experienced a poorly executed upsell at least once in our lives, and realize that it damages the customer relationship.

Your customers can tell when you're interested in them only for the money, not the relationship.

Consider another metric: Economic Value to the Customer (EVC). Economists speak of this number as the maximum that a customer is willing to pay for a solution. EVC is a combination of *tangible* and *intangible* benefits to the customer.

For a subscription customer, the EVC must exceed the cost of renewing. Marketing's job is to increase the economic value as experienced by the customer.

Value nurturing is about increasing the *customer's* perceived value from the solution, not wringing every dollar out of the customer. The better you are at making your customers successful, the more successful your business will be over the long run.

> Revenue growth is the natural result of value nurturing done well.

Lest we let the economists have the last word, cognitive science suggest that the potential for customer happiness is built into the subscription business model itself.

Paying causes us a small degree of pain. We do not enjoy losses, and the moment of paying seems like a loss. (No surprise here.) A subscription replaces many small decisions to pay with one decision—the subscription.

Cognitive science also tells us that once the pain of payment is done, we are free to enjoy the results of our purchase. In the book *Happy Money: The Science of Happier Spending*, authors Elizabeth Dunn and Michael Norton posit that we are happiest when we pay for something up front and then continue to enjoy it afterward. (Once you've paid for that all-inclusive vacation, you are going to savor and enjoy every moment.)

A subscription model in which you pay up front opens the door for sustained enjoyment. Value nurturing is about optimizing and engineering the post-sale experience of value. It's a quest for customer happiness, and it can be a great deal of fun if you approach it creatively.

The Five Big Ideas of Value Nurturing

Just as the word *value* has several meanings, there are at least five distinct approaches to value nurturing.

1. Helping customers find success

People subscribe to your solution for a reason. Maybe they believe it will save them money or make their lives easier. Perhaps it seems entertaining. They expect value in return for subscribing, whether for personal or business use.

The simplest and purest expression of value nurturing is to help your customers realize this value, fulfilling the implicit brand promise of your marketing.

To do this, you may reach beyond the marketing organization, aligning with *customer success management* efforts in the business. Smart subscription marketers are interested in *all* post-sale customer conversations and experiences.

2. Demonstrating value

Once customers start achieving success, marketing can discreetly remind them of the value they're realizing. These strategies range from sending gentle reminders to delivering personalized data. All share the aim of reinforcing the experience of value (tangible and intangible) in the customer's mind.

3. Creating value outside the solution

Creative marketing organizations go beyond merely communicating solution benefits. They add value outside the product or service through content, community, and data.

4. Creating value through the relationship

Subscription success grows from long-term relationships with customers. Marketing organizations can take ownership of tending and nurturing those relationships. Think of these strategies as the "romantic advice" of customer marketing. Find ways to make your customers love doing business with you.

5. Aligning with customer values

Customer loyalty is critical for the financial performance of a subscription-based business, so taking the high road can pay off over time. Businesses that succeed in sharing their customers' values create strong, long-lasting bonds with their customers. Purpose-driven marketing strategies may have growing impact in the years to come.

Choose Your Own Path

The chapters in Part Two present an extensive menu of ideas that you can implement for value nurturing.

Some belong squarely in the marketing domain, while others require collaboration across organizational boundaries. You may be able to implement several of them quickly and easily, but a few require high-level buy-in.

What you do with these strategies is up to you. You may already be doing many of these activities, although reconsidering them as *value nurturing* may change your perspective. If you're practicing a few of these strategies, consider adding more. You probably won't reach a saturation point on customer loyalty.

The final chapter in Part Two is about the free trial conversion. For many businesses, the free trial is that critical moment when lead nurturing ends and value nurturing begins. If you offer any kind of a trial, pay attention to whether you're nurturing the customer experience.

The examples that follow come from all types of businesses, not just subscriptions. Consumer brands like Coca-Cola and rock stars like Lady Gaga alike recognize the value of maintaining audience loyalty. Subscription marketers can learn from many teachers.

Pay attention to the experiences of companies outside your own industry. If you market business-to-business solutions, make sure you read the consumer-based examples with care. You can learn a great deal by looking further afield than your own competition and keeping an open mind. In today's fast-changing marketing environment, stepping outside your comfort zone can yield results.

Part Two

Value-
Nurturing
Strategies

Chapter 6

Create a Customer Launch Plan

There's nothing most marketers love more than a good launch. A product launch, a company launch, a book launch—you name it, we'll launch it. If nothing else, a launch gives us a sense of accomplishment and an excuse for a party.

In all the excitement about the glamorous, high-profile launches, it's easy to neglect the many small but critical events happening all around you—customer launches. Over time, the cumulative effect of these individual beginnings has a larger impact on your business than any media launch event.

If you're looking for the low-hanging fruit of value-nurturing strategies, you've found it. *Something* motivated the person to become a customer. Do what you can to guide people to ongoing success before they lose momentum and forget why they signed up.

Creating a customer launch plan makes sense for almost any business and works equally well for subscription-based and traditional business models. There's almost no excuse *not* to have a customer launch plan. Plus, there are powerful psychological reasons for taking action right away.

Design the launch plan to get customers working with and realizing value from your solution as quickly as possible. An early success feeds the *positive confirmation bias*, or our tendency to look for evidence to support the decisions we have already made.

Immediately after making a choice, we look for signs to confirm that the decision was a good one. As behavioral economist Richard Thaler writes in *Misbehaving: The Making of Behavioral Economics*, "People have a natural tendency to search for confirming rather than disconfirming evidence."

We look for those experiences that prove us right in choosing to subscribe, so the early days of a subscription are a valuable opportunity to supply that confirming evidence.

That's why the "customer onboarding" or welcome experience is so critical. The first interactions confirm that the subscriber made a sound decision to use the service. Because making decisions takes effort, we'd rather not analyze them repeatedly. If we start using the solution with good results, we will probably continue.

Reduce the Barriers to Getting Started

According to ServiceSource, provider of recurring revenue and customer success management solutions, a 90/10 rule applies for new subscribers. If a customer doesn't start using your solution within ninety days, there's only a 10 percent chance they'll become a loyal customer. Although this data may be skewed toward technology solutions, the general concept holds true for nearly all subscriptions. If people don't start using them, the reasons for subscribing may fade from their memories.

Your launch plan might start with a series of emails with links to videos or other useful resources. Give people a way to opt out. Treat every email, every transaction, and each bit of communication as an opportunity to reinforce the reasons for choosing your business.

Have you ever wondered why Apple invests so heavily in packaging design for its products? From the moment you open the box, you sense that you are using something special, and it colors your experience going forward.

You may not be shipping products in a box, but your initial interactions with customers are the metaphorical equivalent. Pay attention to the details of how your customers unwrap and explore the experience.

The customer journey does not end at the sale; rather, the point of sale is where the story starts to get interesting, at least from the customer's perspective.

The first act of nurturing value can be as simple as crafting each step of the setup with care.

For example, whenever you subscribe to an application or email service, you inevitably see a message like: "Check your email for a confirmation link." In the United States, this double opt-in ensures that email subscriptions meet anti-spam regulations. It protects the business by validating that the person signing up for the service is associated with the email account being claimed.

What does that opt-in confirmation email look like to subscribers? What is the tone and style? Do you anticipate any problems that people may have? Where do you send them when they click the link to confirm the subscription? What's the first thing a new customer is likely to want to see?

Walk through the customer setup process, looking for every opportunity to create the right impression and guide the user to the next step.

Welcome Email

Your launch plan might be as simple as a well-constructed welcome email. You *do* have one, right?

I must confess: I sometimes sign up for applications in the heat of the moment, and then don't get started with them. I may forget that I have signed up at all. A well-written welcome email can save the day.

When I signed up for the Haiku Deck service for creating online presentations, I wasn't actually working on a presentation at the time. Months later, I needed to use the service. After searching through my email, I found a welcome letter that refreshed my memory and got me started, including:

- How to log on (and how to reset a forgotten password)
- Links to getting started materials and tutorials
- A link to frequently asked questions

Better yet, the email was written in a conversational, friendly style and reminded me why I had signed up for the service. The welcome email can play a critical role for people (like me) who sign up and then wait before taking action.

Another great welcome example comes from Buffer, the social media sharing and scheduling service. Once I signed up for Buffer's "Awesome" plan, two emails arrived right away.

The first, from the account of co-founder and CEO Joel Gascoigne, welcomed me as a subscriber, setting a personal tone for the ongoing relationship. He also reminded me that *I could cancel at any time.* Not many businesses do that when you first sign up. Simply seeing that statement made me trust the company just a bit more.

The second email was a payment receipt, but here, too, Buffer made the transaction fun and personal, including a picture of the Buffer team at a work retreat. The email ended with this quote: "We will also do our best to provide great value for you day in and day out."

Remember what I said about the job of subscription marketing: earning trust and nurturing value? In its two welcome emails, Buffer declared its intention of doing both. Well done.

The launch plan isn't all about automated emails and online onboarding. Sometimes, the best welcome is personal. The more high-tech your solution, the more powerful a personal connection can be, through email, a phone call, or even a handwritten note.

Automated Onboarding Programs

Technology makes it possible to see what your customers are doing with your solutions and spot whether they're off to a good start or not. When operating at scale, find ways to automatically track usage and adoption. If it looks like the customer isn't succeeding, reach out and see if you can help.

Test the onboarding carefully, with people both inside and outside the company.

If you want to see examples of the good, bad, and ugly of user onboarding, check the "teardowns" published by Samuel Hulick on his site, useronboard.com. I guarantee that you will learn something, and return to look at your own onboarding process with fresh eyes.

Chapter 7

Orchestrate Early Success

The high-end dining business is built on repeat customers and customer referrals. A pricey restaurant cannot succeed unless its customers think that the food and overall experience were worth the investment.

Few restaurants in America have the cachet of The French Laundry in Yountville, California. It boasts three Michelin stars and measures its wait list in months.

Once you walk in the door for your long-awaited reservation, you have committed to the fixed price menu (or *prix fixe*, since it's The *French* Laundry). What does the staff of this famous, "impress your friends by saying you've eaten there" restaurant do? They hand you a tiny appetizer that looks like an ice cream cone, made with smoked salmon and crème fraîche in a delicate wafer.

I haven't been to The French Laundry (*yet*, that is—I am an optimist) but I have heard the chef, Thomas Keller, discuss the role of his famous salmon cone. He calls it one of the most important parts of the meal.

The unexpected and whimsical appetizer serves two functions:

1. The gesture welcomes those diners who may feel intimidated about entering this well-known dining mecca. What better way to break the ice than to give someone a treat that looks like an ice cream cone?

2. The appetizer launches the dining experience with familiar reference points. As Keller says, it tastes like something people have experienced before (salmon and sour cream), so they tend to like it.

From a marketing perspective, this gesture is a customer launch plan rolled up neatly in a wafer: Establish the relationship through a friendly gesture and create the first experience of success.

Look for ways to implant similar early success with your own solutions.

Use Videos to Accelerate Success

If your solution isn't intuitive to use, marketing should make it as painless as possible for customers to get up to speed quickly.

Video can save the day. It's usually easier to *show* customers how to do something than it is to explain it. People can watch videos on their own schedules. Even for relatively easy-to-use solutions, video answers any lingering early questions quickly.

Zipcar has a series of short videos in which a Zipcar "co-pilot" talks people through the processes of getting a car, extending a reservation, fueling the vehicle, and returning it.

None is longer than a couple of minutes, and they remove the mystery for new customers.

Embed Guidance in the Solution

Even the simplest solutions have a learning curve. Your mission is to help customers navigate that curve quickly, reaching the point at which being a customer is easy and rewarding, rather than a difficult cognitive effort.

If software is part of your solution, consider embedding online guides and pop-up help to direct people through the learning process.

Slack is an enterprise messaging and collaboration program that has shifted perceptions about what "enterprise software" looks like by focusing exclusively, even obsessively, on the user experience. From its earliest days, the people at Slack understood that rapid user success was key to its growth. What good is a collaboration tool if you're the only one in your team using it?

In an interview with Kara Swisher on the Re/Code podcast, Slack CEO Stewart Butterfield said that customer success was the company's prime engineering objective: "We focused all of our effort on the new user experience, and I think that's what's made the difference."

This focus carries all the way to the initial login. Instead of an ordinary email confirmation with instructions for logging on, the company sends first-time subscribers a "magic link" to make the first login painless. A cheerful, automated Slackbot helps people with the next steps and offers context-appropriate options, advice, and encouragement.

Don't go overboard with embedded help, though. Remember Clippy, the helpful paper clip in an earlier version of Microsoft Office? Poor Clippy inspired violent thoughts in Microsoft users worldwide. There's a fine line between offering assistance and intruding. Provide an easy way to opt out.

You don't have to build a bot; you could embed tips and suggestions that show up the first few times someone logs on. Or, create a timed email campaign that sends weekly suggestions for the first few weeks after someone subscribes.

Guide Customers Through Critical Milestones

Once someone is signed up, early success campaigns often cross the line into customer success. So, consider this advice from customer success evangelist Lincoln Murphy, describing the three key steps of helping customers succeed at scale:

1.   Identify the good fit customers for your solution.
2.   Identify the *desired outcomes* for those customers.
3.   Orchestrate those outcomes.

(To read more, visit Murphy's site at SixteenVentures.com or read his book *Customer Success*.)

Depending on the complexity of your offering, the customer onboarding process may involve leading customers through multiple steps. Those customers who complete all the milestones will most likely achieve their desired outcomes.

If you've done the work of segmenting customers, you can enroll them automatically in campaigns that lead them through the relevant milestones. If you aren't sure which track someone should be on, proactively offer them the chance to enroll in the "start-up plan" that meets their objectives. Flesh it out with training, checklists, and personal assisassistance where required.

The work you invest in orchestrating the initial customer path pays off in subscribers who stick around.

Chapter 8

Help Customers Create New Habits

If your solution requires people to change their behavior, you have the opportunity to influence customers as they shape new habits.

As director of the Persuasive Technology Lab at Stanford University, B.J. Fogg researches how to use technology to change behavior. The Fogg method, as he outlines it, consists of three steps:

1. Identify the specific behavior you want to occur.
2. Determine a small step toward this final goal, and make it simple: the easier the behavior, the greater the chance of it becoming habit.
3. Trigger this behavior through prompts or environmental changes.

Technology can aid with habit formation by providing a "trigger" or reminder for these behaviors. But behavior can be stubborn, and you should not take it for granted that subscribers will immediately change the way they do things, no matter how wonderful your solution is.

Guide New Customers Through the Habit Change

Meditation is like exercise; making the time to do it each day is a challenge. For the online meditation app Headspace, the challenge isn't explaining to people how to use the app; it's getting them to make the time and meditate regularly.

Headspace eases potential customers into the meditation habit by offering a free course of ten days, ten minutes each, called the "Take Ten" program. Once you subscribe, the company sends a welcome letter with useful links and instructions, encouraging you to complete the ten days. At the conclusion, emails prompt you to continue with a paid subscription and additional meditation courses. You can opt in to meditation reminders or ask to be connected with a meditation buddy.

Getting the reminders right is a delicate balance. As a business promoting mindfulness and inner peace, the last thing the company wants to do is to irritate its subscribers. By guiding people through the start of a meditation practice and supplementing the software with reminders and social support, Headspace influences habit formation.

Encourage New Habits with Gamification

A little friendly competition can serve as additional motivation when forming new habits. That's why fitness trackers suggest that you share your data with others and include competitive and game-like features.

Gamification is adding elements of traditional games (points or badges, competition) to other, non-game activities, making them more fun or habit-forming. Many businesses use gamification to encourage adoption and loyalty.

For years, I carpooled to chorus rehearsals in San Francisco with three other singers. Being Silicon Valley denizens, we relied heavily on navigation applications like Waze. As we sat in traffic or wound our way through back streets in San Francisco, we would track our progress, keep track of the changing arrival time, and report slowdowns and accidents back to the app. Reporting observed incidents earned the Waze users commuting points that eventually led them to achieve *ninja* status.

For Waze (now part of Google), customers who share their real-time experiences make the data itself richer and more valuable for all Waze users. It's the *network effect* in action, in which each addition to the network increases its value overall. Providing points for participation encouraged the Waze subscribers to use the app, delivering more data and increasing loyalty.

If gamification can improve the experience of commuting in traffic, then it's on to something.

From a value-nurturing perspective, adding a competitive or gaming component may encourage customers to use your solution so they realize value quickly.

Chapter 9

Offer Great Training

With solutions like enterprise software, long-term success may require customers to develop expertise. Learning becomes part of the adoption hurdle. Make sure you offer effective, accessible instruction for subscribers.

Training programs represent a golden opportunity for marketing organizations to influence the customer's realization of value. Remember that Economic Value to the Customer, or EVC, is the sum of the tangible and intangible value perceived by the customer. For complex products, effective instruction is one of the surest ways to increase the tangible value of your solution.

Interestingly, effective training can also move the needle on the *perceived*, or intangible, value. As customers invest time and effort in learning, their personal commitment to your solution increases.

If you do a terrific job of teaching them, people are more likely to become loyal customers.

Choose Training Based on Customer Needs

Design and present the training in the right formats and doses to match the customer's needs.

For example, in the business software world, administrators or power users may seek out intensive instruction, while everyone else can get by with a few videos. You may develop several training tracks, divided into short, functional components that people can access at the right moment in time. If you offer live webinars, also publish the recording after the fact for those who cannot make the scheduled time.

We are surrounded with diverse options for on-demand learning and instruction in our personal lives; your customers will expect you to provide a similar range of options. Offer training through multiple formats, such as videos, podcasts, and written materials. For directed or assisted training, consider using a learning management system.

Add Value through Certification

Amplify the impact of instruction by offering formal certification for those who complete in-depth training.

Certification gives customers explicit evidence of their skills and makes the solution more valuable as part of their skillset. Many technology leaders offer certification training, including Apple, IBM, Google, HubSpot, and countless others. Technology companies know that certified practitioners become powerful advocates, particularly in industries in which people change jobs frequently.

Chapter 10

Share Customer Stories

Businesses often rely on case studies or customer success stories as lead-nurturing content to move prospects through the sales cycle. Marketers love them because they offer essential *social proof*—the sense that since others are doing something, it must be worthwhile.

Customer stories can also play an important role in value nurturing. If you're already creating these stories, use them to enhance the *perceived value* delivered to existing subscribers.

Share Customer Stories with Your Subscribers

Although marketing organizations ask existing customers to participate in case studies, we often forget that they may also be interested in *receiving* them. These stories are potent illustrations of how others have achieved success. They may remind customers of the benefits they are seeing, or inspire them to do more.

You probably already spend time developing customer stories to attract prospects and generate leads. Sending them to current subscribers takes little added effort. Think of this strategy as a free trial of value nurturing, using content you already have at hand.

- When a customer first subscribes, send them relevant stories.
- When you first publish a customer story, share it with existing customers.
- Actively solicit your subscriber base for other examples of great stories or interesting applications.

This value-nurturing campaign gives you an opportunity to start conversations with your subscribers. You may find people doing interesting things with your solution, who are willing to share their own stories.

As a member of the discount warehouse Costco, I receive the monthly *Costco Connections* magazine, where the company profiles many of its small business members. In addition to providing useful content, the magazine showcases the members and their activities. Profiling current customers is a great way to add value to subscriptions.

Let Customers Tell Their Own Stories

What happens when someone stands ups and tells their story, either in person at a conference or virtually in a blog post or customer piece?

By speaking out, those customers become advocates for your business. They internalize and "own" their success as a customer. You've given them a showcase for their expertise and the opportunity to assist others.

Customer stories are one component of *advocacy marketing*, or getting loyal customers to testify on your behalf.

Can you think of ways to expand beyond your traditional, marketing-driven "customer success story" program to solicit stories from people in their own words?

The Zendesk blog includes a series of posts tagged "Story Room." In these posts, customers tell their own stories, either through an interview or by directly submitting a written post.

Could you do something similar?

You might dedicate part of the blog for the customer voice, or create a customer-only area of a website for people to share their experiences. It could be as simple as an online community or a social media page. Invite customers to share their experiences with others.

Chapter 11

Quantify Your Value

The fastest way to demonstrate value to a customer is to do the math for them. Put a number on the tangible or intangible benefits of a subscription.

Supermarkets use this technique regularly. When I check out at the local Safeway using a loyalty card, the cashier tells me how much I saved while handing me the receipt, addressing me by name. The transaction includes an *immediate* and *personalized* assessment of the monetary value of subscribing to their loyalty program. (I pay for my subscription to this loyalty program with data, not money.)

We live in a data-driven world, so you're probably already collecting all kinds of data. See if you can use it to nurture your customer's experience of value.

Demonstrate Value with Customer Usage Data

Activity monitors tell us how far we have walked, sleep monitors track how long and deeply we slept, and the utility company reports how our gas, electric, or water usage compares to our neighbors. Most of us are pretty comfortable with the concept of usage data at this point.

Chances are that you're collecting usage data about your customers that could reinforce or strengthen the customer's perceived value. Try to convert usage into measures of the benefit to the subscriber: time saved, healthy meals prepared, blog posts published, or whatever is appropriate for your business.

Even if you're already providing that data in reports, guess what? Not everyone runs or reads the reports. Consider making that effort for them on occasion.

If the value that your solution delivers isn't monetary, you may need to be creative to put the data in context or make it interesting.

Many companies send "year-end wrap-up" emails that put usage data in a fresh context. For example, I received a year-end report from the ride-sharing service Lyft, presenting data for the year, including my total rides, miles traveled, and other stats, as well as "badges" that I have unlocked. (The badges are a gamification strategy.) It was a pleasant reminder of the times I used the service, and its value to me.

Aggregate Value Across All Your Customers

Perhaps you cannot easily pull personalized data for each individual customer. Maybe your service is such that it seems intrusive to deliver personalized data. One of the cardinal rules of value nurturing is this: Don't be creepy. You don't want customers to feel that you're stalking them.

Do you remember that story about Target extrapolating from buying patterns which of its customers were pregnant, and sending baby-related coupons to those shoppers? That didn't work out well for the teenager who hadn't yet told her parents about her situation. When data mining algorithms are too good, you can creep out your customers.

Anything health related has the potential to be creepy, particular if you're *not* in the healthcare business.

In these situations, it might be safer to aggregate data across all your customers rather than sharing individual information. When using aggregated data, be careful to remove any indicators that would betray individual customer's data or usage.

ThreatMetrix is a digital identity company that helps financial and enterprise customers protect online sites and customers from malicious actors. The company publishes a real-time visualization of the threats detected and blocked across its global network. Red dots appear on a world map showing the instance and severity of account takeover, payment fraud, and identity spoofing attacks foiled by ThreatMetrix technology, without identifying its customers.

Sharing this information demonstrates value to current customers as well as prospective ones. The company also shares quarterly cybercrime analysis reports with the industry.

Whether you're providing individual usage or aggregated data, you'll remind subscribers of the reasons for remaining customers, and perhaps spur them to do more with your solution.

Chapter 12

Celebrate Successes

I joined my first start-up when it was just a handful of people. The vice president of sales put a small gong on his desk. Whenever we signed a deal, he struck the gong, so everyone within earshot knew. In the early days, we were *all* within earshot, since the office was quite small. As the company grew, the gong-striking celebration continued, setting off minor celebrations and shared congratulations.

Celebrations keep us going through long hauls.

As your business grows, look beyond your own sales and achievements to find reasons to rejoice. The successes that will fuel your long-term growth belong to *your customers*. The more your customers achieve with your solution, the better for your business. When you take a moment to celebrate with them, you acknowledge and reinforce your partnership.

> When customers experience success with your solution, applaud that success without claiming the glory.

Build Celebration into the Experience

In some situations, you can engineer celebration into your solution.

MailChimp, the email marketing service, makes it quick and easy to create and send email campaigns. But hitting the Send button on your first email campaign can be nerve-wracking. MailChimp takes the pressure off by showing a giant, animated chimpanzee finger hovering nervously over a button. The moment you send the campaign, the chimp hand gives you a virtual high-five.

It's funny and charming. But it's also an acknowledgment that by sending the mail, you've met one of your goals for using an email marketing solution. MailChimp celebrates with you.

Honor Continued Usage

You don't want to be one of those companies that only reaches out to customers when selling something or raising prices.

A celebration is a great reason to contact a loyal or continuing customer—someone who's not reporting problems and might otherwise be neglected. Look for small victories in customer usage data.

Fitbit sends badges to celebrate certain milestone achievements, such as a maximum number of steps taken in a day, or lifetime distance covered. One day you may receive an email telling you that you have walked the entire length of Italy or India. This serves as a reminder of what you have achieved together. The company doesn't claim the glory, but celebrates it with you.

Personal Emails

Like many independent authors, I use various Amazon services in the course of publishing my books, including its CreateSpace print-on-demand service for paperback editions.

With the exception of an occasional newsletter, most emails I receive from CreateSpace are transactional in nature, telling me about the status of a draft or shipment. So I was surprised to find a message congratulating me on the inclusion of one of my books, *The Writer's Process,* on a list of the best self-published books of 2016. Someone on the CreateSpace team took the time to send wishes for continued success. It made me feel like more than simply an anonymous customer.

This simple gesture of celebration was a powerful example of value nurturing in action.

Chapter 13

Create Value Through Content

Creative marketers add value beyond the solutions they market, through compelling content.

Marketers are great at creating content—it's what we do. Supplement a subscription offering with content that customers find useful. This content might take the form of blogs, papers, ebooks, social media posts, books, and magazines, graphics, videos, podcasts, or other media.

As David Meerman Scott writes in *The New Rules of Sales and Service*,

> Once someone is signed up as a customer, information delivered at the right moment makes for a happy customer who renews existing services and buys more over time. And happy customers talk up companies on social networks.

Take the content marketing strategies you use before the sale and extend them after the customer signs up. Continue to deliver value through content, and customers will remain engaged.

The content has to be valuable in and of itself. It cannot simply promote your product or toot your own horn. Think of ways to serve your customers.

For inspiration, read Jay Baer's book *Youtility: Why Smart Marketing is About Help, Not Hype*. This quote from the book sums up his general approach: "If you sell something, you make a customer today; if you help someone, you make a customer for life."

Online and Offline Publications

Using content to create value is a long-standing marketing strategy exemplified by businesses that publish magazines— the printed kind. AAA publishes a travel magazine (*Via*) as a complement to its insurance and roadside-assistance offerings. Charles Schwab sends an investment magazine to its customers. If your business only interacts with customers intermittently, a content subscription increases loyalty and reinforces value.

The quality of a print publication can become a growth engine, spurring community participation and support. The quarterly magazine *First & Fastest* is a publication of the Shore Line Interurban Historical Society, a group of railroad buffs based in the Indiana/Illinois/Wisconsin tri-state area. Rail enthusiasts beyond the society's Midwestern origins value the quality of the content and print production. The magazine publishes a lengthy list of "sustaining subscribers" who pay more than the baseline subscription fee to support the publication. According to content-marketing expert and *First & Fastest* subscriber Roger C. Parker, "When you deliver exceptional quality on a consistent basis to a targeted market, the support will appear."

While print magazines still serve many subscribers, more content distribution happens online. Many brands create online hubs combining written, graphic, audio, and video content, offering media for every preference. These sites become preferred destinations for customers looking for more than product information.

Birchbox provides its subscribers with a monthly box of personalized health and beauty product samples. To differen tiate itself and add value, Birchbox also publishes an online magazine filled with content related to health and beauty.

The site includes articles and instructional videos that help customers get the most value from their subscription boxes. The content goes beyond what's in the box. Interviews with authors appear alongside articles on how to keep your shirt from coming untucked (spoiler: use tape).

As another example, consider Adobe, a company I've already highlighted for its pivot to the subscription model. Adobe publishes an online site, CMO.com, for chief marketing officers and marketing professionals.

The site's editors curate useful articles, news, and podcasts about marketing and develop original content on trends and predictions. CMO.com does not pitch Adobe Marketing Cloud; rather, the company delivers valuable content for current customers as well as prospects. The content hub serves multiple marketing purposes, including brand awareness and value nurturing.

Tune In to Podcasts

Podcasting has taken off in recent years. If you want to generate content regularly without a great deal of writing, podcasting is one way to go. Better yet, it's got a subscription model built in.

According to Edison Research, the number of Americans listening to podcasts is growing steadily, rising 23 percent from 2015 to 2016. Look around you. Those people you see on your commute or plugged into headphones at the gym may well be listening to podcasts.

A podcast can serve existing customers and prospects alike. According to a survey of 1,000 podcast listeners, conducted by Edison Research and the Interactive Advertising Bureau, nearly two-thirds of podcasting fans would consider buying products or services they hear about on podcasts.

To be effective as a value-nurturing strategy, any podcast must obey the laws of content marketing by providing information that is useful, educational, or entertaining. Consider creating a podcast series by interviewing people your customers find interesting. Profile customers. Have your in-house experts talk about trends affecting customers, or share tips about improving their businesses.

Consumer brands, media companies, and business brands like Oracle and IBM use podcasting, and the number of podcasts is growing nearly every day. You won't reach all your existing customers with podcasts, of course. There's only so much time in the day to listen to content, and you have to earn the audience attention. But for customers who love listening, a podcast is a great way to make a personal connection and to repurpose content you are already sharing in other formats.

The best podcasts feel like personal conversations, bringing the listener in closer to the brand or strengthening a relationship. Plus, once recorded, podcasts are "evergreen" and continue reaching people with your content.

Turn Data into Valued Content

Many online businesses collect large volumes of operational data. That data may be valuable to your customers.

For example, Netflix displays a list of which movies are popular in my hometown. It doesn't cost them much to share this nugget of data with me. If I discover a movie or television show through this feature, then that bit of insight has increased the value of my Netflix subscription.

The ride-sharing service Lyft publishes "The Lyftie Awards" for the most visited restaurants, hotels, transit stops, and tourist destinations worldwide, as well as regional listings for restaurants, bars, and event venues. These awards are a clever way to offer valuable insight based on data that's already been collected as part of doing business.

Similarly, ride-sharing service Uber gathers data about traffic patterns as part of its daily operations. The company is analyzing and sharing that data for the public's benefit. Through Uber Movement, the company strips identifiable information from the data, aggregates it, and makes it available to city planners, municipalities, and the public, delivering value to the communities it serves.

For a company occasionally caught in contentious legal situations as it pioneers a business model, returning value to communities through data is a great idea.

Create Entertaining Content

Businesses often use humor as a way of getting attention from the world at large and attracting customers. Remember the Old Spice "Smell Like a Man, Man" videos? These funny clips exposed a mature brand to an entirely new demographic. The most entertaining Super Bowl commercials often get more buzz than the game itself.

But humor and entertainment play a serious role after the sale as well, keeping customers and subscribers engaged. Some brands are simply fun to do business with. I open their emails and visit their websites because I know that I will enjoy the experience.

Dollar Shave Club launched its subscription grooming products business with a hilarious video that went viral: "Our Blades are F***ing Great." That video earned the start-up a great deal of attention. Once a subscriber signs up, the barely suitable humor continues with a monthly "Bathroom Minutes" newsletter that accompanies the box and is filled with articles like "Which Body Parts Can You Actually Grow Back?" and others I won't quote here.

Beyond earning attention, being funny can sustain the long-term customer relationship.

Humorous content doesn't belong exclusively to consumer goods. Adobe produced an amusing video in which marketing mishaps delay a rocket launch, as part of its "Do you know what your marketing is doing?" campaign. Humor can work in many markets if it is appropriate for your brand voice.

Alas, being hilarious is easier said than done. You cannot predictably plan to have a campaign go viral. However, you can leave room for humor or a light touch in your customer interactions, like the flight attendants on a Southwest Airlines flight who communicate the safety features of the aircraft with humor. If you can't make people laugh, try to make them smile.

For inspiration, check out the book *Stop Boring Me! How to Create Kick-Ass Marketing Content, Products and Ideas Through the Power of Improv* by Kathy Klotz Guest, which applies the principles of improvisational comedy to marketing.

Chapter 14

Create Community

Connecting people in meaningful ways is an act of generosity. Businesses that make connections add value to their customers' lives. While competitors can copy your solution offering, duplicating your community is much more difficult.

Businesses are waking up to the power of community around their solutions. Many software-based subscriptions integrate social commenting, sharing, and messaging to increase the social value of the product. But that's not an option for every type of subscription.

If you can't easily fit social features into your product, the marketing team can find ways to create community *outside* the solution.

Build Communities on Social Media

Many businesses create and manage customer communities on social media sites like Facebook or LinkedIn. If your subscribers spend time on these sites, then by all means cultivate relationships there.

However, on Facebook and LinkedIn, your community is subject to the changing rules of the platform. Also, with everything else happening on those platforms, your business presence may get lost in the noise. Earning a place in your subscribers' news feeds can be difficult.

You may achieve better visibility and participation by staking out a place in a more targeted social media platform. The Right Margin, a goal-driven writing tool, has found success by carefully building and developing a Slack team dedicated to writers, called WriterHangout.

Like many technology start-ups, The Right Margin started out using Slack internally to collaborate. The team then had the idea of creating a writing-related team on Slack for writers, existing customers, and beyond. The Writer-Hangout team quickly grew to an active, participatory community.

The Right Margin team maintains a hands-off approach to WriterHangout, participating and encouraging without taking over or directing conversations. When customers sign up for the Right Margin service, they receive a welcome email also inviting them to the Slack team.

The Slack community has helped the young company reach a broad number of writers early in its lifespan. One thread (or *channel* in Slack terminology) in WriterHangout is dedicated to The Right Margin service. This channel serves as a kind of help desk and sounding board for the product teams. The company tests feature ideas, solicits input on potential user interface changes, and gets a better idea of what people want and need through the personal connections forged in the online community.

But this Slack community is not about sales or prospecting. The other WriterHangout channels cover topics that the writers want to pursue: submissions, rejections, contests, short stories, book marketing, etc. Many participants make personal connections, communicating through private, direct messages within the platform. The community has become a place where people connect and support one another, which was The Right Margin's purpose from the start.

"Although we want to use it as an extension of what we're building with The Right Margin, we're really glad to see that we're adding value to a writing community," says Will Sullivan, the vice president of marketing for the company. "Supporting writers is essential to our brand promise. If we can do that, even outside the product itself, then we're succeeding."

Branded social media communities only work if you commit to participating in and nurturing them, without exploiting them. This means contributing useful content, responding to any service issues, and answering questions promptly.

Create Your Own Virtual Communities

Some businesses go further by creating communities on their own sites, or so-called "owned media" in contrast to sites owned by Facebook, LinkedIn, and others.

American Express has always positioned its customers as *members,* implying a sense of community and inclusion. When pursuing small business customers, the company goes the extra mile by running its own virtual community, known as OPEN Forum.

OPEN Forum gives American Express members a place to ask questions and share information with other small businesses. Editors post selected articles on technology, leadership, marketing, and finance. The company calls it a forum for *exchanging* advice. This community adds inherent value to the American Express card membership.

In-Person Gatherings

Connections made at in-person events are often stronger than those made online. Salesforce is deeply committed to virtual communities, but it also hosts one of the largest in-person gatherings in the technology industry, the Dreamforce conference. According to the Salesforce blog, more than 170,000 people attended the conference in 2016, with an additional 15 million people joining for streaming video.

Salesforce pulls out all the stops at these conferences. Past lineups have included famous musicians (Bruno Mars, U2), politicians (Hillary Rodham Clinton), and inspirational speakers (Tony Robbins).

Why the major push around a physical conference for a company that prides itself on being entirely cloud-based? Through the in-person conference, Salesforce builds and strengthens relationships with customers and partners. Attendees realize a sense of belonging and community. If the event didn't pay off, I doubt the company would continue to invest in hosting it each year.

If a conference sounds too staid for your business, consider emulating Red Bull.

Subscription companies can learn from creative consumer goods companies that live or die by repeat purchases and brand differentiation. As a consumer beverage company, Red Bull counts on people repeatedly making the decision to buy and drink its product. Each additional purchase is a kind of subscription renewal. (The company also has a subscription magazine—the *Red Bulletin*—so you *can* actually subscribe to Red Bull.)

Many major brands compete for market share in the energy drink business. Red Bull makes loyal fans by connecting them with a community, both online and at sporting events. Visit the Events section on the Red Bull website, and you can find an event happening on any weekend, in multiple locations around the world. Samples include:

- Ski and snowboard "open jam" competitions
- Off-road racing and road rallies
- Ice cross downhill racing (this sounds crazy)
- Art fairs
- Music festivals

Red Bull sponsors most of these events, labeling many with the Red Bull brand. Participants and observers alike become part of the Red Bull community merely by showing up. Customers meet and interact with other people who share their love of extreme sports. How's that for adding value?

Chapter 15

Nurture Your Fans
and Advocates

Loyal customer advocates generate leads by referring your business to others. They talk to the media and analysts when asked and participate in customer testimonials, providing valuable credibility for your business.

Advocacy marketing is the practice of nurturing and developing the fans and advocates in your base. Done well, advocacy marketing is a prime example of value nurturing. Done poorly, it can backfire.

Given their potential value to your business, use caution when soliciting advocates and customer referrals. In a rush to build a lengthy list of referrals, businesses can antagonize the people they most want to nurture.

Your challenge is to turn subscribers into fans and fans into advocates, while sustaining the trust you have earned and delivering real value to those fans and advocates. Marketing teams and customer success teams work together to develop campaigns and programs to:

- Recognize loyal customers and potential advocates, such as people who proactively reach out with comments or advice for others
- Reward advocacy through recognition, exclusive access, special programs, or simple thanks
- Give advocates the support they need to operate effectively on your behalf

Find Your Fans, Superusers, and Potential Advocates

Evangelists, superusers, advocates, heroes—whatever the label, you want more of them. These are the loyal subscribers who go beyond simply staying and using the solution. They spread the word to others.

> A superuser or advocate is a subscriber who is loyal to the point of action.

In the business-to-business context, the superuser may accelerate adoption within a larger account, answering questions for others and demonstrating how the solution applies locally. In the consumer market, an advocate may be the customer who tells friends or influences others.

The trick is finding those people in your customer base who are loyal to the point of action. One way is to look for behavior that suggests a loyal fan with a tendency to refer. These may include the following:

- Subscribers who are active or sophisticated users of the service
- Customers who share recommendations on social media platforms
- People who submit reviews or suggestions for new features
- In the B2B context, individuals in a role that affects a large number of other users

Try to identify loyal fans and advocates through their behavior and reach out proactively.

For example, loyal customers often leave reviews, and leaving reviews correspondingly increases loyalty. Amazon frequently asks you to review products you have purchased from the company. When you submit a review, Amazon thanks you for *helping other customers*. If another shopper marks the review as useful, Amazon lets you know. This is one way of reinforcing the behavior of people who contribute reviews.

In other cases, loyal fans may appear if you create programs to attract them, such as bonus points for referrals.

Adagio Teas uses both approaches, offering opportunities for advocacy and rewarding those they discover. I am a fan of the company's teas and order from them repeatedly. Whenever I place an order, the order page includes social media referral links, which customers can share to earn loyalty points.

The day after Christmas I placed an order. (Emergency holiday tea shortage!) To my surprise, I received the tea the next day. Because I was so delighted with the speedy service,

I sent out a tweet. Adagio thanked me (on Twitter) and credited my account with loyalty points.

Notice how this worked. The company monitored Twitter to find my referral. The loyalty points were a gesture of thanks. I did not send the tweet for money or points, but the company rewarded me for the action after the fact.

That leads to my main point, and the place where advocacy programs can go awry:

> Advocacy should be earned, not bought.

Reward Advocacy

A company I've never heard of sent me an email recently, offering to pay me for subtly mentioning the company to my email list, without making it seem like an endorsement or advertisement.

I said no.

They were looking for *paid* advocacy, not earned advocacy. The company hadn't earned my trust ahead of time. I trusted them even less when they requested that I not mention that they were paying me to my subscribers.

Paid advocacy raises all kinds of issues. In the United States, the Federal Trade Commission has published disclosure guidelines for bloggers and others who promote or endorse products or services in blogs, social media, or advertisements. If you're paid to recommend a product, come out and say so.

Offering money for referrals or advocacy is a slippery slope for other reasons as well. It doesn't always make sense from a psychological perspective.

Behavioral psychology reveals that paying people for completing tasks (such as a referral) can actually *reduce* their motivation to act by replacing an intrinsic or internal motivation with an extrinsic one. In his book *Predictably Irrational*, Dan Ariely describes studies in which researchers paid MIT students varying fees to complete puzzles. Ariely found that increasing the monetary compensation *decreased* performance for tasks requiring cognitive skills.

If you are delighted by a service and tell a friend about it, you have done something generous for both the friend and the company. It feels good, and that is your reward. If the company offers to pay you $10 for every friend you tell, the act of referral seems cheapened. The payment puts a dollar value on your action, changing it to a commercial transaction instead of a personal one. That can have several negative effects:

- You may feel that it's not worth your time. ("Ten bucks? That's all my endorsement is worth?")
- If you make the referral for money, you lose the satisfaction of acting on someone else's behalf.
- If money is tight, you may refer everyone you know, cheapening the strength of the referral.

You want to encourage customers to refer your business because they are taking a positive action for others, not only for financial gain. Money is rarely the best way to incentivize brand advocates and referrers.

Don't worry, there are other means.

Don't underestimate the power of a personal expression of thanks. If a customer has said kind words on social media or referred someone else to your business, take the time to offer thanks, whether through a handwritten note, a follow-up call or visit, or other gesture. Handwritten notes are pretty rare these days, and can make a major impact.

Sending a gift as an unexpected thank-you *after* a referral doesn't pose the same danger as offering payment ahead of time. In the business or government context, make sure to check whether the recipient works for an organization with policies against accepting gifts.

Perhaps you can reward the advocate with experiences rather than money. For example, give customer advocates special treatment or access to events they find valuable and interesting.

To scale up your advocacy efforts, create programs to develop, support, and recognize the advocates among your subscribers.

Advocacy Programs

Well-designed advocacy programs benefit everyone:

- The advocates receive recognition, additional resources, and the overall satisfaction of assisting others.
- Newer customers benefit from having a variety of people available to answer their questions and provide guidance.
- Your company benefits from increased customer loyalty and success.

Hootsuite is a social media management dashboard. The Hootsuite Ambassador program combines free training, exclusive access and promotions, and online recognition, plus the ability to claim membership with an Ambassador badge. The additional layer of membership adds value to the customer experience for the company's Ambassadors.

Salesforce calls its most loyal customers MVPs. Salesforce MVPs are expert in the software, answer other customers' questions, and are willing to be brand advocates. But that's not enough to earn MVP status: other customers or Salesforce employees must nominate you for this award, and customers can hold the title for one year only.

Salesforce recognizes and supports the MVPs with elevated status in the community, invitations to speak at events, access to exclusive networking events and product briefings, training, and certification, and Salesforce MVP–branded shirts and things (swag).

Notice that both Hootsuite and Salesforce include training and education components, making advocates more effective at helping other customers.

Chapter 16

Ask for Advice and Input

Have a new release coming out? Want input on a marketing campaign? Ask your customers for advice, whether for product direction or marketing messaging.

Many businesses invite customers to serve on advisory panels and solicit their opinions about features or services. Not only do you benefit from the insight of your customers, but you'll also strengthen your relationship with people who enjoy being helpful.

Customer-Generated Content

When coming up with content for campaigns, consider fielding contributions from your existing customers. Babson College deployed this strategy with its multiyear campaign around the definition of entrepreneurship.

Babson positions itself as the educator for Entrepreneurship of All Kinds™, with business programs for undergraduates, graduate students, and executives. In 2012, the school reached out to its community and beyond to crowdsource definitions of entrepreneurship, collecting contributions on a page of its own website.

The school kicked off the campaign using paid media to invite people to participate. Current and prospective students, faculty, politicians, business leaders, and alumni all submitted ideas. The school collected thousands of definitions, which it used to create marketing and branding campaigns.

Inviting community participation extended the school's reach beyond what it could otherwise influence with traditional outbound marketing. The campaign drove more than two hundred thousand visitors to the Define Babson site, with unique visitors from 182 countries. According to Sarah Sykora, Babson's Chief Marketing Officer,

> We have been using our limited marketing dollars to engage our community and the market to share our message for us. Their reach is greater than our spending would allow, and third-party sharing is much more powerful than us talking about ourselves.

The campaign served several purposes:

- It created awareness of the college among the broader population (lead generation). Sykora reported that the number of inquiries about Babson's entrepreneurship programs increased at all levels (undergraduate, graduate, and executive education).

- For prospective students, the campaign reinforced the school's commitment to entrepreneurship (lead nurturing).

- It infused existing staff and faculty with a sense of shared mission and pride (employee engagement).

- For alumni, the campaign forged a sense of community, potentially strengthening ties to the school (value nurturing).

That's a marketing quadruple play. The college later expanded the campaign by inviting the global community to offer definitions of social innovation.

By welcoming and encouraging customer and community participation, you will strengthen the ties between your business and its customers. As Simon Mainwaring writes in his book *We First: How Brands and Consumers Use Social Media to Build a Better World:*

> The most effective way to attract consumers today is to invite them to share and help shape your brand narrative. Brands are finally starting to notice that loyal consumers want to be part of their brand's storytelling.

Let the Customers Guide the Product

Pley.com is part subscription box, part sharing economy, and completely delightful. The company offers monthly boxes of toys to keep (like a subscription box) as well as subscriptions to rent educational toys from the company's extensive toy library.

Pley.com started out with LEGO® sets using a Netflix model. Parents (or anyone who enjoys assembling these creations) can subscribe to receive a set each month, complete with extra pieces and instructions. When it's done, they can send it back and get another.

To support and nurture the subscribers (parents and children alike), the company created a separate community called PleyWorld in which customers submit their own designs for LEGO creations and vote on the designs of others. When a design receives a critical number of votes, the team at Pley creates instructions and offers it for rent or purchase through the Pley service.

It's a brilliant way of encouraging participation, community, and creativity among its users. The PleyWorld mission, according to the site, is "to democratize the creative process and empower builders across the world to be Master Builders." By developing and nurturing creativity in the subscriber base, the company strengthens the loyalty of those customers. And, it keeps its product line fresh and dynamic with these crowdsourced designs.

Chapter 17

Handle Breakups Gracefully

Even in the best of situations, customers leave. Let them go gracefully. They may return if you handle the departure well.

The marketing organization should write the end-of-life plan for customers; leaving this moment to chance is risky.

Have an Exit Plan

We've all heard horror stories about people struggling to cancel subscriptions. Worries about ugly breakups can prevent prospects from subscribing in the first place.

It's creepy to cling to a customer who's trying to leave. By all means, find out why they're leaving and try to address any problems they have. But then let them go with dignity. They might return.

You might even proactively reach out to inactive subscribers to services or emails and offer them a chance to leave. I loved the "invitation to unsubscribe" email I received from Return Path, experts in email deliverability and optimization. After asking me politely if I wanted to continue receiving the emails, the message offered me a simple choice: Click on the happy koala to stay, or the sad monkey to leave.

Return Path unsubscribe image

Even if you unsubscribe, you do so with a smile.

Welcome Returning Customers

When happens when you resubscribe to a business you've left?

- The business might treat you like a new customer. You probably aren't insulted, but you do feel forgotten.
- You may be pleasantly surprised to find that the business welcomes you back and acknowledges the past relationship.
- Customer-centric subscription businesses let you make up for lost time or pick up where you were before you left.

This third approach may promote ongoing loyalty from intermittent customers.

If a former customer restarts a subscription, welcome that person back like an old friend. Don't make them start at the beginning. For example, create a welcome back campaign with content that varies based on how long they've been gone. Think about what returning subscribers need, and guide them to rapid reentry.

My son Mark introduced me to the value-nurturing activities of Blizzard Entertainment, makers of the World of Warcraft®, Diablo®, and StarCraft® games. Mark was an avid gamer in high school, but stopped playing (thankfully) in college. On summer breaks, he would drop back into the online games.

Many gamers probably follow this pattern; bursts of active use followed by periods with less time for gaming. Blizzard makes it easy to rejoin the gaming world if you've been gone for a while. When you leave, your account is frozen rather than deleted. If you sign up after an absence, the company connects you with resources that help you start having fun quickly, including:

- A Returning Players Guide: The online guide includes account management, major game changes, new features, and the latest updates so returning players can find out what's happened in the online world in their absence.

- Character-level boosts: The company uses the occasion of new releases (expansions) in the online world to offer incentives for preordering, such as the "level 90 boost" that shortcuts the hard work of "leveling

up" a character in the world. These incentives often
lure back inactive users.

These resources serve the purpose of getting the returning player engaged and playing again as quickly as possible.

Chapter 18

Share Your Story

When a customer subscribes, your business becomes part of *their* story. If you both believe in the same things, your role in their personal narrative expands. Companies that align with their customers' deeper values earn ongoing loyalty.

In his book *True Story: How to Combine Story and Action to Transform Your Business,* Ty Montague suggests, "People don't buy products; they take actions that help advance their own personal metastory, and sometimes buying and using your product is one of those actions."

Venture capitalist Ben Horowitz suggests that crafting the company story is essential to business strategy. In an interview published in Forbes, he said:

> The mistake people make is thinking the story is just about marketing. No, the story is the strategy. If you make your story better, you make the strategy better.

Your story and your values are inextricably linked. What is the history and mission of your business? If the purpose and values aren't immediately clear to people inside and out, your first task is to identify shared values that the entire business can rally around.

The most powerful stories and values align closely with the core business.

For example, Dawn dishwashing liquid prides itself on cutting through grease on dirty dishes. It's also effective at cutting through oil on marine mammals and sea birds. For decades, Dawn has donated dishwashing liquid to The Marine Mammal Center and International Bird Rescue for cleaning wildlife affected by oil spills. It publishes videos of volunteers washing baby ducklings with Dawn dish soap. Who doesn't love baby ducklings? In the process of supporting an environmental cause, Dawn reinforces its brand identity and solution value.

In the business world, software giant SAP offers free online courses on sustainability through its OpenSAP online training platform. In 2014, Peter Graf, then the Chief Sustainability Officer for SAP, led a class titled "Sustainability and Business Innovation." In the course, Graf shared his experiences working within SAP, with its supply chain, and with customers to set and report on sustainability goals.

More than 14,000 people took the course worldwide. The company has since updated the class and added other offerings, including a class called "Sustainability through Digital Transformation" and a weekly podcast, Sustainability Snippets.

These resources, offered freely to customers and others, advance the company's goals. By affecting the behavior of its customers, SAP multiplies the impact of its environmental and social sustainability efforts. (The company's customers include most of the world's large manufacturers.) SAP reinforces its role as a partner in innovation and supply chain accountability.

Both Dawn and SAP chose campaigns aligned with their solutions and stories. Their values-based actions are tightly integrated with the brands themselves.

Values-Based Marketing Requires Commitment

Corporate values must extend far beyond the marketing organization. In the best-known, often-cited examples of values-based businesses, the commitment starts at the level of the CEO.

Under CEO Paul Polman, Unilever has built social impact and environmental sustainability into its core value propositions. The company sets aggressive goals as part of its Unilever Sustainable Living plan, and promotes those goals on its website and in its corporate reporting. For example, by 2030, the company's goal is to halve the environmental footprint of people making and using its products. That includes customers!

The company reports annually on its progress toward its Sustainable Living goals. This *isn't* a marketing campaign—it's a corporate strategy.

Many familiar household products are part of the Unilever family. Marketing organizations in those brands create campaigns that are consistent with the parent company's vision and story. For example, Sunlight (makers of dishwashing liquid) has joined with Oxfam to provide communities in rural Nigeria a sustainable source of clean water for household uses.

Patagonia is another example of a business with values-based leadership. The founder, climber Yvon Chouinard, shaped the company's commitment to the environment. Patagonia makes headlines by encouraging its customers *not* to buy its jackets unless they really need them. That's a truly revolutionary stance for a retailer.

Patagonia treats its customers like subscribers, prolonging the customer relationship to reduce its environmental impact.

- The company repairs items that customers bring in to the stores.
- Customers can trade in gear that is still in good shape, which will be resold as used through the Worn Wear® program. This program highlights the durability of Patagonia goods.
- Patagonia recycles any clothing and gear that cannot be resold, keeping those materials out of landfills.

Both Unilever and Patagonia are committed to a common purpose, from the CEO through marketing and operations. While CEO engagement is important, nearly every business can find ways to act on issues that its customers and employees alike care about.

Communicate Your Values with Customers

Once you have agreement on your business values and story, communicate them effectively. Exactly how you do that will depend on your business's story and brand personality.

BarkBox has a simple story: A bunch of dog lovers create a subscription service for dog treats. The company's self-declared mission is to make dogs happy, and its "About Us" page features pictures of employees with contented canines in the workplace.

BarkBox donates 10 percent of its profits to animal shelters, rescue organizations, spay and neuter programs, and other dog-related nonprofits. It shares its values (love of dogs) with customers, and acts on those values in a way that is consistent with the company story.

As Ann Handley says in her book *Everybody Writes*:

> At its heart, a compelling brand story is a kind of gift that gives your audience a way to connect with you as one person to another, and to view your business as what it is: a living, breathing entity run by real people offering real value.

Invite Customers to Participate

Find ways to work together with customers in support of their higher values.

When a massive earthquake struck Nepal in 2015, Facebook posted a Donate button, working with International Medical Corps to raise and distribute aid to the devastated country. The company matched every dollar of the first two million dollars donated. Facebook users joined in, raising more than $15 million in a week in addition to the $2 million pledged by Facebook. The company invited customers to participate, and participate they did.

Dick's Sporting Goods used a similar cause-related marketing strategy to support youth athletics in the United States.

A sporting goods business depends on people of all ages participating in athletic endeavors. Through its charitable foundation, the company created a Sports Matter campaign in early 2014 to raise awareness of the funding crisis in public school sports and assist teams raising money for their operations.

The campaign included videos, social media, and celebrity endorsements. Dick's also sponsored an inspirational documentary, *We Could Be King*, about two rival Philadelphia high schools facing budget cuts.

Through the campaign, 187 teams in thirty-five states raised the money to operate. The Dick's Sporting Goods Foundation provided matching funds of $2 million, doubling the amount raised through local fundraising.

Do you wonder whether those fundraisers, team players, and parents are loyal fans of Dick's Sporting Goods now? I don't. I suspect that they will return to Dick's repeatedly, with positive feelings about the purpose of the company.

Caveats with Values-Based Marketing

The values-based marketing strategies described above can misfire if you aren't careful. Before you start down this road, beware of the ways that you can go astray.

First and foremost, you cannot fake your values. The best marketing campaign will hurt you in the long run if your business isn't genuinely committed to the story and values you espouse.

In his book *The Big Pivot: Radically Practical Strategies for a Hotter, Scarcer, and More Open World*, Andrew S. Winston argues that with today's technologies and our interconnected world, businesses must realize that transparency, not secrecy, is the new normal. As Winston writes, "The power of big data and transparency is a relentless tide." If you don't align corporate behavior with stated values, eventually the world will catch on.

One of my favorite stories of radical transparency doesn't come from the world of business at all. The U.S. Supreme Court will sometimes edit opinions that they have already issued. This practice wreaks havoc for legal scholars who rely on the originally published opinions, only to discover that the law of the land is slightly different. The Supreme Court only sends records of these changes to a few paid subscription services.

To address this situation, V. David Zvenyach, counsel and part-time coder, created a simple application that crawls the Supreme Court website for changes and publishes them through a Twitter account (@SCOTUS_servo). All it took to bring transparency to the Supreme Court edits was a simple script and a Twitter account.

What does this mean from a business perspective?

Make sure your company story is legitimate. Remember BP's "Beyond Petroleum" campaign? BP's relatively minor alternative energy investments were overshadowed by the company's aggressive efforts pursuing oil reserves. Claiming environmental values you do not embody leaves you open to accusations of hypocrisy.

Make sure you have high-level buy-in for any values-based strategies you deploy.

Additionally, beware the *curse of purpose*, or weighting social or environmental virtues more heavily than your prospects do, while neglecting other customer values and requirements.

All things being equal, people want to do business with companies that share their values. This fact doesn't give you permission to ignore quality, functionality, or price. Whole Foods may sell organic food, but its customers don't sacrifice shopping experience or product quality. If you lead with environmental or societal value, it should *enhance* rather than replace the solution value.

Chapter 19

Embed Values in Your Business Model

When it comes to aligning with customer values, the strongest positions belong to those companies that embed a greater purpose in the business model itself. Values and business become inseparable.

You can embed purpose into the way that you sell the product or into the legal structure of the business.

Products with a Purpose

Toms Shoes built its business with the vision of providing shoes to children in need around the world. According to the company story, Blake Mycoskie saw children in rural Argentina going barefoot and wanted to do something about that situation. He started Toms with the premise that for every pair of shoes sold, the company would donate a pair to a child.

Through the Toms One for One® model, the company has given more than 35 million pairs of shoes. Every customer participates directly in the company's story through the very act of being a customer.

Over the years, the company has extended the One for One model to products beyond shoes:

- For every pair of sunglasses sold, the company donates eye exams and glasses to those in need.
- Toms couples coffee purchases with donations toward clean drinking water in the countries where the coffee beans were grown.

The company's mission and purpose enriches the value of the products they sell. As a customer, you don't simply buy shoes; you buy the knowledge that as you wear the shoes, a child elsewhere now has a pair of shoes as well.

At the end of the year, Toms sends a thank-you video describing the cumulative effect of this business model. In 2016, that effect included 14 million pairs of shoes distributed and 115,000 vision-restoring treatments.

Other businesses have embraced a similar model, including Warby Parker for eyeglasses and Bombas for socks.

What if you're working with an established business not built around this kind of mission? You can embed purpose into existing offerings.

During flu season, Walgreens promotes its Get a Shot. Give a Shot® campaign. When a customer buys a vaccination at Walgreens, the company donates money to provide vaccines to children in developing countries, working through the United Nations Foundation.

The Walgreens example is proof that you don't have to be a scrappy start-up to integrate purpose into the fabric of your business model.

The B Corporation Movement

A growing number of companies are embracing the concept of the *triple bottom line*, which encompasses people, planet, and profits. Businesses that embrace social and environmental purposes earn a serious competitive advantage by aligning with customers' deeper values. As Simon Mainwaring says in his book *We First: How Brands and Consumers Use Social Media to Build a Better World:* "The future of profit is purpose: Consumers want a better world, not just better widgets."

Customers are rewarding these shifts. According to the 2015 Cone Communications Ebiquity Global CSR Study, consumers expect companies to operate responsibly, and they seek out responsible products when possible.

Some people argue that purpose and business don't mix. In publicly traded businesses, management and board members have a fiduciary responsibility to protect the interests of shareholders. With public markets pressuring businesses for short-term, quarter-by-quarter performance, the profit motive can lead to decisions with negative long-term consequences.

A growing number of businesses counterbalance the profit motive by adopting a legal structure that includes social purpose. These are *benefit corporations*.

In the United States, a benefit corporation is a for-profit entity that includes benefiting the public as part of its legally defined goals. Profit motives are balanced with the public good in making decisions, and the businesses agree to report on these objectives.

The benefit corporation movement is growing. In the United States, state-by-state rules for these entities vary. Around the world, countries are considering or adopting their own versions of benefit corporations.

A nonprofit organization, The B Lab, certifies businesses based on social and environmental performance, public transparency, and accountability. As of the end of 2016, the list of Certified B Corporations™ included more than 2,000 companies in fifty countries.

Of course, it is easiest for companies that are just getting started to incorporate as a benefit corporation, so the list of Certified B Corporations skews to smaller businesses. But a few established companies have also adopted the model, including Ben & Jerry's (a subsidiary of Unilever), Patagonia, and Natura (a publicly traded Brazilian cosmetics company).

These are profit-based businesses working to make a difference in the world.

When purpose is embedded in the business model in this way, it withstands changes of management at the board or executive level. Customers who choose to do business with B corporations know that something larger than a profit motive informs the relationship.

I expect to see this model grow in coming years, particularly as the subscription trend continues to gain hold and ongoing customer relationships become ever more vital to business viability.

Chapter 20

Nurture Free Trial Users

The free trial is a critical part of the sales process for many subscription businesses. Trials give the prospective customer an opportunity to try out a solution before signing up.

The trial isn't just about what's in the box or part of the solution. It's about the experience.

| A free trial is a chance to evaluate the experience of being a customer.

When selling a subscription solution, marketing organizations have two key objectives: demonstrating value and earning trust. Many of the value-nurturing strategies in this part of the book have involved demonstrating or adding value. But do not neglect the importance of earning the customer's trust.

Before undertaking a long-term relationship with your business, prospective subscribers want to know they can trust you. They will ask themselves questions like:

- Is your business going to stick around once they've invested in working with you?
- How careful will you be with their data?
- Can they trust you with automated payments?
- Will they find more success in their personal lives or jobs by subscribing?

The free trial is a test of your ability to earn and maintain customer trust. However, organizational issues can get in the way of these objectives.

The Free Trial No-Man's Land

The free trial customer is not completely a prospect, nor entirely a customer, but a little of both. That dichotomy leads to problems. For example: Who owns the trial user relationship? How much do you interact with that prospect? What will those interactions look like?

Some businesses take a hard-sell approach to the trial: The sales and marketing team engages under full steam, and the trial customer experiences the electronic equivalent of the used-car sales lot experience, with persistent emails, phone calls, or chat boxes popping up.

Other businesses adopt a "hands-off" approach, treating the trial users like current customers, assuming that anyone having a problem will contact customer support. Or, they hand off customers to customer success teams for onboarding as if they were paying customers.

But the trial user is not necessarily the same as a new customer—not yet.

People often sign up for a free trial before they are ready to make a purchase. They might use the free trial as a way to learn more before making a decision. The customer success teams should not have to shoulder the burden of following through on the marketing message at this stage.

If you've read this far and believe in value nurturing, then you recognize this important fact:

> The free trial is when lead nurturing becomes value nurturing.

Start applying the concepts of value nurturing to help trial customers achieve an early success. Call on the strategies described in this section, and work with sales, support, and customer success teams to nurture the trial subscribers. For example:

- Provide training resources, videos, or email campaigns to encourage trial customers to discover the features that will provide the most value. (If you have segmented customers, you'll have a better idea of where to steer the prospect.)
- Observe the trial user's online behavior and trigger campaigns, emails, or phone calls if people appear to be lost or off-track.
- Offer assistance periodically (but not with annoying insistence) during the trial.

Remember, the trial is an opportunity to earn the prospect's trust and demonstrate what this relationship will be like going forward. Don't nag and annoy, but be ready and responsive.

Free Trial vs. Freemium

Take care not to confuse a free trial with a freemium (short for "free/premium") model.

With a free trial, people can use the solution for a fixed time, then they are expected to convert to a paying subscriber or depart.

In contrast, businesses using a freemium model expect that a large number of customers will remain unpaid subscribers, while a smaller percentage will upgrade to a paid offering immediately, and others eventually convert as their needs grow.

If you execute a freemium model successfully, those free users amplify your marketing reach. They will be so delighted with the free version that they become advocates, recommending your service to others. For example, the Evernote application captures and shares online notes across devices. The application grew rapidly through avid fans of the free version of the software; it appears everywhere on bloggers' lists of favorite productivity tools. The customers of the free version became the application's most outspoken advocates.

The freemium model can be a wonderful growth strategy, but it requires careful planning. Remember, your overall goals as a subscription marketer are to demonstrate value and earn trust. For the freemium model to achieve these goals, the following must be true:

1. The free version has sufficient value in and of itself. It should not be a "gutted" version designed to get everyone to convert.

2. There is enough differentiation between the paid and free versions so the value of the paid version is evident.

3. You know how many paid users it takes to support the overall platform.

4. The model is financially sustainable, so you do not have to back out features or capabilities from the free version because you cannot afford to deliver them. Once people have gotten used to something, they are unhappy to lose it. Entitlement takes hold quickly! Removing features or functions from existing users violates their trust.

The Moment of Conversion

If all goes well, many trial users will convert to paying customers. But not *all* will, even for the most effective trials. Your optimal conversion rate may depend on how well you target your marketing.

Never take the conversion from a trial user to paid subscriber for granted. The way that you handle the conversion to a paying customer can either add to or detract from the customer's experience.

For example, many businesses collect a credit card at the start of a trial, and begin billing after thirty days. This approach has many benefits: It filters out the prospects who are not yet that serious and simplifies the conversion when it does happen.

But when the moment comes that you are ready to bill the customer the first time, do you go ahead and post the charges? Or do you remind them? Even if you have the customer's financial information or first payment in hand, ob-observe the moment of conversion with care.

If the customer has forgotten about the trial and discovers an unexpected charge on a credit card, you've just eroded a bit of trust from the relationship. That does not bode well for long-term loyalty.

I use Rainmaker Platform to run my author website. When I signed up for the free trial, I gave the company my credit card.

During the thirty-day trial period, Rainmaker provided a huge amount of training in various formats, including videos, written guides, webinars, and guided tours. The company did not try to "sell" me once. When I had a question, the support team answered it promptly.

Three days before the end of the trial, the company sent me an email that began like this:

"We're writing because in about 72 hours, your trial access to Rainmaker will be ending and your first payment will be processed."

The email included links to login information and additional resources I could use to get going. It also offered individual assistance if I needed it. But here's the most important thing: By reminding me of the pending conversion, the company gave me implicit permission to cancel the payment if I wasn't happy or ready. By doing so, the company earned my trust—trust that has been reinforced over the long term.

The trial was a terrific model of the ongoing customer experience.

There's a postscript to this story: I so enjoyed experience of being a customer that here I am, recommending the product to others. Value nurturing done well leads to loyalty and customer advocacy.

Part Three

Putting the Strategies into Action

Chapter 21

The Business Case
for Value Nurturing

I hope that by now I've convinced you of the role of value
nurturing and you have found strategies you'd like to implement. Now it's up to you to convince the rest of your
organization. This chapter should give you the necessary
ammunition to do that.

The Hard Numbers Behind Customer Value

The word *nurturing* sounds like something that only a liberal
arts major would love. But you can justify it using revenue
numbers.

If you have to build a case for value nurturing, find out
if your business tracks any of the following metrics:

- Customer retention
- Customer (or revenue) churn rate
- Customer loyalty (Net Promoter Score® or other
  measures)
- Average revenue per account (ARPA)

- Average customer lifetime value

Any of these metrics can supply the foundation for a business case.

Retention and Churn

Customer retention and customer churn are two sides of the same coin. No matter which way you track them, value nurturing should have a major impact on churn and retention.

I'm an optimist, so I like to think about retention. But if you want to get someone's attention, talk about churn. First, a little terminology:

- Customer churn refers to the rate of customers who leave (don't renew or unsubscribe) in a given period of time.

- Revenue churn refers to the reduction in revenue over a period of time.

The two are linked, but not equivalent. If your current customers go through hard times and scale back their subscriptions, they remain but revenue drops. If some of your current customers love what you do so much that they upgrade or buy other services, the increase in revenues can offset a loss of customers.

For simplicity, we'll talk about customer churn for now. If you can make a measurable difference in customer churn rates, you can have a major revenue impact over time.

Most businesses have a natural churn rate, representing customers who leave for ordinary reasons having nothing to do with the business. For example, customers of a diaper delivery service usually churn when the blessed day arrives that the child stops using diapers.

Any churn above and beyond that natural rate represents lost revenue.

Because retention and churn compound over time, relatively small, incremental improvements result in major revenue differences. Think of it like cumulative interest in a retirement account; small percentage changes make a huge difference compounded over decades.

Assume that your annual customer retention rate is 85 percent and you have 1,000 customers. Without adding new customers, at the end of four years those 1,000 customers are down to about 522—just over half of what you started with.

If nurturing efforts improve customer retention to 90 percent (cutting annual churn from 15 to 10 percent), you'll have 656 of those original customers at the end of four years.

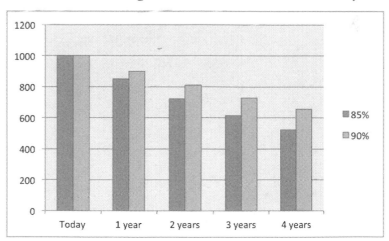

The difference between 85 and 90 percent retention

These numbers don't include any customers you acquire in the interim. As your retention rate rises, new customers represent *growth* rather than replacement. They become part of a higher baseline for the next year's customer retention rate.

Start-ups may not worry about churn in their early days because attracting customers seems relatively easy. In a fast-growing start-up with $100,000 in annual revenue, replacing $10,000 lost to churn seems quite doable. Your eyes are on the first million, not that $10,000.

The larger your business grows, the more difficult it becomes to replace subscribers who leave, simply because the numbers grow larger. When revenues reach $10 million annually, you would need to find a *million dollars* of new business to replace revenue lost to a 10 percent churn rate. That's just to stay even, not grow—and investors want growth.

How can value nurturing change those equations?

- By helping customers realize the value from their subscriptions, effective value nurturing reduces customer churn.

- Value nurturing also creates a fertile environment for cross-selling and upselling, reducing revenue churn. You may be able to expand revenues from existing customers enough to offset revenue losses from customers who leave.

Improving Customer Loyalty

Loyal customers stick around. They are the first to try out new features and services and tell you what they think. They recommend the service to others, providing highly qualified leads that convert quickly.

A loyal customer is a growth accelerant.

Businesses use many tactics to measure customer loyalty, including monitoring behavior and conducting surveys.

The Net Promoter Score (NPS®) is one of the most common metrics for tracking loyalty. This metric quantifies loyalty through customer responses to a single question: How likely is it that you would recommend [this company] to a friend or colleague?

Advocates of the Net Promoter Score claim a correlation between the score and overall business performance and market valuations. Even without assigning a dollar value to NPS points, everyone would agree that customers who recommend your products or services are economic assets. Word-of-mouth marketing is basically free. Leads referred by existing customers cost you less to acquire than other leads and tend to convert more quickly.

A successful value-nurturing program should improve measures of customer loyalty or satisfaction. When customers realize the value they achieve through your subscription, they are more likely to recommend it to others. If you do a good job of demonstrating value to customers, they can share that information with others more easily.

If you track NPS, you could use this score to prove the effectiveness of your value-nurturing program. Otherwise, track the number of leads referred by existing customers. Customer advocacy and referrals demonstrate of the power of value nurturing.

Increasing Customer Lifetime Value

How much is a customer worth in revenue to your business over time? What would happen to your revenues if you increased average customer lifetime value by 5 or 10 percent?

The math behind customer lifetime value gets complicated quickly if you dig into the details. But in general, a customer's lifetime value depends on three variables:

Spending: How much the customer spends each period (monthly, yearly)

Margin: How much is left after the cost of serving that customer each period

Churn: The probability of the customer leaving

Effective value nurturing increases customer lifetime value in multiple ways:

- Practices that promote rapid success reduce the likelihood of customers leaving early in the life cycle. Subscription customers who repeatedly renew become more valuable over time.

- Customers who realize significant value from your solution are much more likely to either upgrade or extend their use (responding to upsell campaigns or offers). They are also more open to other services you offer (cross-selling). Both of these behaviors increase revenues.

Customer lifetime value is a predictive, forward-looking measure. While value nurturing should increase customer lifetime value, its initial effects will be visible in current or backward-looking metrics like retention and average revenue per account.

Focus on Revenue Opportunity

One way to reframe the financial discussion around marketing priorities is to look at marketing spending in relationship to overall *revenue opportunity* rather than gross revenues.

You could rightly argue that marketing should spend time and money on areas with significant revenue *potential* as opposed to current revenues.

The revenue potential of your existing customer base depends on:

* The subscription price paid by the customer
* The average length of time a customer remains a subscriber
* The customer's potential for churn (churn rate)
* The potential for expanded revenues (upsell and cross-sell rates)

The more mature your business, the larger the potential revenues from existing customers. Compared with new customers, these revenues have no up-front acquisition costs. A small investment in customer value nurturing protects and increases potential revenues.

Overcoming Objections

Customer value nurturing is an *additional* marketing task, not a replacement for what you're doing already. You never get permission to stop generating leads, building awareness, or doing any of the other tasks that drive revenues today. As a result, value nurturing may be a hard sell in marketing organizations already feeling pressured by competing demands.

Every good marketer learns to address sales objections. In that spirit, here are a few arguments to address the objections you might encounter.

Objection: "Our subscription offering is new, so we have to put all our resources into lead generation."

It's hard to argue with the importance of lead generation, especially for new offerings or start-ups. However, given the cumulative effect of customer churn on growth, the best time to start value nurturing is on day one. With fewer customers, you have the opportunity to test and fine-tune your strategies going forward. The steps you take in the early days establish a culture in the marketing and sales organizations of serving the customers after the sale.

Objection: "Management wants to see subscriber growth, so we really need to focus on lead generation instead of customer marketing."

Remember that it's much less expensive to keep and develop existing customers than to acquire new ones. Reducing churn effectively boosts growth by ensuring that customers you do acquire aren't simply replacing ones that leave.

Objection: "But marketing is compensated on leads generated, and sales is compensated on net new sales. No one wants to spend time on current customers."

This is the most insidious objection of all: The system is rigged against value nurturing. When that's the case, it's time to re-rig the system.

Return to the metrics at the beginning of this chapter: churn, retention, loyalty, and customer lifetime value. Find ways to incorporate those measures into broader performance metrics for the company, its executives, and even the sales and marketing teams. For example, many customer success experts recommend that sales compensation should de-depend on loyalty, with a full commission paid only when a customer renews.

If you want to create a culture of long-term customer relationships and value, you have to align incentives with those objectives.

Chapter 22

Start Nurturing Value

You already have many of the skills. You've read through the list of strategies in Part Two. You've built a business case. What's keeping you from implementing a value-nurturing practice right now?

Even if you haven't convinced others, you can choose the easiest, low-hanging strategies: the customer welcome plan, sharing customer stories. Finesse them into your marketing plans. If you choose this "act first, ask for permission later" approach, measure and track your results so you can expand your efforts.

Here's some advice for adding value nurturing to your standard practices.

Take the Marketing Inventory

Which strategies you choose will depend in part on your current marketing style and practices.

The modern marketing professional must be familiar with an overwhelming array of trends, tools, and strategies.

Any investments you have already made in marketing technologies and skills will influence your approach to nurturing subscribers. Ultimately, the *customer* should be the guiding motivator behind your choice of strategies.

For your first campaigns, choose the strategies that match existing marketing skills and strengths. Take an inventory of what you are already doing with content marketing, social media marketing, and marketing automation. Look for easy ways to expand those efforts to reach customers beyond the initial sale.

Content Marketing

Content marketing is about creating content that your prospects and customers want and need, at any phase of their relationship with you. It is the driving force behind several of the strategies, such as adding value through content.

Content marketers apply a disciplined approach to creating content that meets specific prospect and customer requirements. The practice requires an understanding of the following:

- Who are you trying to reach? Content marketers develop specific buyer personas to better understand and target their efforts.
- What are their specific needs and questions?
- Where do they seek help for those needs?

Having answered those questions, create useful resources for each point of their journey with you.

If you have developed customer personas, then you're already thinking about what your customers want and need.

Helping them realize success after the sale isn't a stretch. Value nurturing adds content and tasks to your objectives.

Rather than focusing solely on supporting the sale, create content that delivers value to existing customers after the initial sale. According to Joe Pulizzi, founder of the Content Marketing Institute and author of the book *Epic Content Marketing*: "Goals to keep customers longer, happier, and/or spending more are the most noble content marketing objectives."

Social Media Marketing

Social media plays a role in many of the strategies: helping subscribers find valuable content, creating communities where people can interact, and strengthening relationships.

Most businesses have social media presences on the "big three" platforms: LinkedIn, Facebook, and Twitter. Many post videos on YouTube, or create public teams on Slack. The "right" social network to use for business is the one where your customers spend time.

However, a social media presence isn't enough to build community. It's what you *do* with that presence that matters. The companies that experience the greatest success on social media run innovative campaigns and strategies that their customers find worthwhile.

Social media can also extend the reach of your subscriber-focused efforts. For example, if your plan is to build a sense of community through in-person events, social media networks expand the coverage and reach of those events.

Email Marketing and Marketing Automation

Many of these subscriber-focused strategies rely on email marketing and marketing automation to operate at scale. For example:

- Automate a customer launch plan using a drip email campaign starting at the moment of purchase.
- Use marketing automation to discover when a subscriber is spending hours on a customer support forum. Then trigger an automated outreach or ping a customer success manager.
- Track a subscriber's overall usage or adoption of key features automatically: Trigger targeted, personalized campaigns to lead them past hurdles or encourage adoption.

Automation isn't the answer to everything, but it can free up time that you can use to make personal connections.

Your First Value-Nurturing Campaign

If it feels strange to direct your marketing efforts to current subscribers, start small and expand.

Choose a strategy to run as a pilot program and evaluate what happens. This first campaign serves as a study in shifting your marketing focus to existing customers. Use this project to build cross-departmental participation, create processes to track performance, and learn what works.

1. *Choose an easy, low-cost project for your first campaign focused on current subscribers.*

Part Two describes a wide range of value-nurturing strategies. Choose one that fits easily into current marketing operations and expertise.

2. Define what success looks like and how you will measure it.

Identify specific metrics based on the selected campaign. For a training video, track how many customers click through to watch it and whether that changes their behavior. If you're building value through community, monitor customer engagement. While revenue growth and customer retention are your ultimate objectives, choose metrics that you can track immediately.

3. Experiment and learn from your pilot program.

Use the pilot program to test messages and learn which strategies are most effective for specific customer segments.

If you're adding value though content, for example, try multiple formats (video, papers or reports, audio) and see which ones generate the most interest. If sending emails, use A/B testing of subject lines to discover which issues trigger a response from customers. Approach the process with a willingness to learn.

Measure and Optimize Your Nurturing Strategies

Track the performance of your efforts during the pilot and beyond. Because value nurturing competes with lead generation for marketing time and resources, be ready to demonstrate its effectiveness. As you shift your marketing focus beyond the initial sale, adopt corresponding metrics to monitor your success.

If you made the business case for value nurturing using *revenue, retention,* or *customer loyalty* measures as described in the previous chapter, use related metrics to track performance.

Of course, many factors contribute to measures like churn and loyalty. Some are far beyond the reach of marketing campaigns. And you may not see measurable results of your campaigns for months. Find faster ways to evaluate the effectiveness of your marketing campaigns.

For example, you might track customer engagement with content, blog comments, social media shares and mentions, click-throughs, or content downloads.

You may also be able to correlate customer behavior with campaigns, such as:

- An uptick in usage of specific features
- Increased adoption (for example, a growing number of active users in a business)
- Referrals from current customers

Whatever strategy you choose, measure how it performs in relation to the overall objectives.

Roll It Out, Strategy by Strategy

How many value-nurturing strategies should you deploy?

Deploy as many as you can that make sense for your business and its customers.

The strategies outlined in Part Two often interconnect. Starting with one leads you to the next logical choice, if you put yourself in the perspective of the subscriber.

For example, let's say you've decided to send customer stories to your existing subscriber base. You find stories depicting representative or high-value use cases, and send them to your subscribers. Check one value-nurturing strategy off the list.

Now look at that from the customer's perspective. A subscriber might want to know how she could use the solution in the same way. What kind of additional content could you provide to guide her?

If you're selling software, for example, work with your customer success teams to create follow-on content that answers questions or provides instructions. You might create a video, an online tutorial, or a webinar with the profiled customer. Assist your subscribers in taking the next steps, and you'll be on the path to becoming a value-nurturing master.

Chapter 23

Build Organizational Support

If you've been paying attention up to this point, you may think that the word *marketing* in this book's title is misleading. Helping customers find and realize success requires participation and cooperation from many groups in the business, including sales, billing/account setup, operations, consulting, training, shipping, customer success, and customer support.

To paraphrase the famous line from the movie *Jaws*, "We're going to need a bigger marketing boat."

The successful subscription marketer collaborates with individuals throughout the organization.

Who Owns the Customer Experience?

The core practices of value nurturing extend beyond the marketing organization. Marketers need to collaborate with customer success teams and other parts of the organization. Everyone is responsible for the customer experience.

From the customer's perspective, your business is a single organization. Yes, of course they realize that many people work there, and that they interact with different individuals for billing than for fulfillment or support. Employees may sign emails with their own names.

Yet somehow customers expect consistency. Crazy, huh?

Think of your own experience. Are you annoyed when you get inconsistent answers from two people at a company? Have you ever felt a subtle shift in the relationship from the period before the sale to the days and weeks afterward? Are your calls returned or emails answered as promptly? Does the story remain the same?

When you experience a disconnect or hear conflicting stories from different groups, what is your gut reaction? Do you think, *They must be suffering from interdepartmental communication issues?*

Probably not. More likely, you think, *That company is ripping me off*, or *They're not very competent, I wonder whether I can trust them.*

Many of us spring to the worst possible conclusion first, unless the business has already earned the benefit of doubt.

Every missed handoff damages trust.

Customer Success

If your business has one, the customer success management (CSM) organization is the first place that marketing should visit in its quest to implement value-nurturing strategies. The practices aimed at early subscriber experiences often belong in the domain of customer success teams.

Marketing and customer success should be best friends and close allies. Otherwise, bad things can happen.

The discipline of customer success management has grown rapidly in recent years, particularly in B2B and software businesses. According to the definition offered on the Customer Success Association website, customer success management is "an integration of the functions and activities of Marketing, Sales, Professional Services, Training, and Support into a new profession to meet the needs of recurring revenue model companies."

By this definition, customer success teams take on marketing responsibilities.

Individual customer success managers often work with small groups of accounts to offer personalized support. But this personal approach doesn't work well across tens of thousands of subscribers. To operate at scale, customer success teams deploy traditional marketing techniques. They do this either by working with the existing marketing organization or building their own marketing capabilities.

Irit Eizips is Chief Executive Officer for CSM Practice, a consulting firm that works with customer success teams in varied industries. Eizips has observed first-hand the many ways that customer success teams manage the challenge of scaling. She says, "When you have tens of thousands of subscribers, you cannot possibly hire enough CSMs to affect adoption or advocacy in a personalized, high-touch way. You need someone with marketing chops."

Sometimes the marketing and customer success groups work together well; marketing creates campaigns in collaboration with customer success to aid adoption or encourage advocacy. But organizational barriers and budget constraints can impede this type of collaboration.

For example, if marketing incentives are based on lead generation, those teams are less likely to allocate budget to nurturing the existing customer base. When marketing doesn't step forward, customer success teams hire in-house operational expertise to run email automation campaigns to reach subscribers at scale. Sometimes customer success teams use separate email marketing or marketing automation software, creating silos of customer data and interactions.

Silos are never good for the customer or, in the long run, your business.

Eizips sees this situation gradually changing as businesses realize the critical importance of building collaboration between marketing and customer success.

Customer success and marketing teams can collaborate along many dimensions of the ongoing subscriber experience:

- Identifying and promoting successful use cases among the subscriber base
- Identifying and supporting potential advocates among customers
- Creating email-based "playbooks" for feature or solution adoption
- Sending automated emails to mark milestones in the customer journey, such as the completion of onboarding

You can start with simple efforts, such as collaborating on emails. CSM teams might run email campaigns or customer events past marketing to ensure consistency of tone, style, and message. Or, marketing can provide customer success managers with announcements of new features to send directly to subscribers. This collaboration benefits everyone: The CSM remains the primary contact for the customer, and customers are more likely to open, read, and act on the emails that come from a person they know. For example, Eizips has found that webinar invitations coming directly from a CSM's email address lead to higher open rates and webinar attendance.

Structural Changes

In many ways, start-ups have the easiest path to successful, long-term subscription relationships, because they do not have to break through organizational divisions that have hardened over the years.

In a start-up, everyone wears many hats and gets to know one another, often because offices are so small that you cannot help it. You hear firsthand everything that happens, from crisis to celebration. Immediate, shared goals and close physical proximity make it easier to collaborate across traditional divisional lines and to maintain a shared view of the customer.

But as they grow and build out teams and groups, the turf wars can begin. So, it's best to start with a culture of cooperation between groups. For existing organizations, reworking the way teams operate can be challenging, but I have seen large companies executing well on behalf of the ongoing subscriber relationship.

Here are a few ways that forward-thinking companies are creating the structural foundations for ongoing value nurturing and subscription success.

Embedding marketers in other groups

In wartime, embedded reporters carry the stories of what's happening on the front lines to the world at large. In the battle for customer loyalty and advocacy, an embedded marketer can go beyond reporting, playing an active role in gathering customer feedback and generating customer success stories.

Embedded marketers in customer success teams can create proactive, "low-touch" campaigns that align with marketing messages to enable customer success activities across large subscriber bases.

Cross-reporting

Where does your customer success live in the organization chart? Does it report to a sales executive? Marketing? Customer support? Is it considered revenue-generating or a cost center?

There is no single right answer, but if marketing and customer success reside in separate branches of the organization, building collaborative efforts will be more difficult.

Some businesses address this issue by creating a revenue-focused C-level role, the Chief Revenue Officer. In a subscription-based business, customer success wields a major impact on overall revenue and would probably land in this domain.

Having someone on the customer success team participate in marketing team meetings and initiatives will strengthen the links between marketing and customer success, creating a culture of nurturing customers after the sale.

Customer-focused incentives

The fastest way to institute structural change is by examining the incentive structure. Incentives are a strong statement of corporate culture and values.

If you reward marketing teams based exclusively on net new sales, then in the end, that's what they will focus on, to the exclusion of existing customers.

Consider aligning performance incentives and measures with the customer experience rather than department-specific metrics. For example:

- Sales compensation linked to how long a customer remains subscribed
- Marketing performance judged not only on net new sales but also customer loyalty and retention
- CSM incentives based on overall customer retention and advocacy, beyond their specific accounts

You will have to work with your teams to determine an effective incentives structure for your business. Focus on goals that represent the customer experience and reinforce, rather than discourage, cross-department collaboration.

Process Changes

Structural changes require a high-level commitment that you might not have. Organizational changes are not the only path to subscription marketing success.

Take a page from all those "how to hack your life" articles and figure out how to hack your processes to support ongoing value nurturing.

Businesses of any size or type can think creatively about small process changes that make a large difference in overall attitudes. Here are a few strategies that might work in *any* business:

Create cross-functional teams for specific purposes

I hear what you might be thinking: No one wants to belong to another committee or have another meeting. But as the customer experience spans many parts of the organization, people from different groups should be involved. If you don't want to set up a perpetual, regular group, convene teams around specific objectives relevant to value nurturing, including:

• Onboarding or customer welcome plans

• New feature rollouts

• Voice of the customer/customer feedback

Shadow colleagues in another department

This could occur as part of a new employee training: Have a marketing hire spend a week alongside a customer success manager, a week in sales, and a week in fulfillment to get the sense of the subscriber issues and experience. It doesn't have to be a week; a few hours a day might suffice.

Put every employee through the rotation at least once, and schedule refreshers if the business environment changes.

Invite colleagues to your meetings

If you're implementing a value-nurturing initiative that would benefit from the insight of customer success, support, or sales teams, invite them to weigh in *early* in the planning process. Asking them to sign off at the end, without input early on, can exacerbate any communication problems.

Reset Your Mindset

Successful subscription marketing, with value nurturing, derives from a relentless focus on the customer. As you nurture advocacy among your customer base, you must also become an advocate for the customer.

Just as every marketer must think of the subscriber after the sale, so every customer service manager must maintain a marketing mindset.

Sarah E. Brown, Head of Customer Marketing at ServiceRocket, says "There is no post-sale." She imagines herself wearing a marketing hat as she gathers customer input and "Voice of the Customer" research for ServiceRocket, which offers training, implementation, and support for software companies.

ServiceRocket hosts webinars for existing customers and prospects at the same time, inviting prospects to listen in to the questions and experiences of current subscribers. According to Brown, webinars, podcasts, Ask Me Anything (AMA), and other activities provide value to customers while inspiring prospects to better understand the value of subscribing.

Even the location of office fixtures can redirect attention and adjust mindsets. Unbounce is a software platform that creates effective landing pages for marketers. As VP of Customer Success at Unbounce, Ryan Engeley is laser-focused on customer experience and retention, and advocates for the customers within the rest of the company.

His customer success team has created automated, visual dashboards that display current data about the customer experience, installing them in common areas on each floor of the company's headquarters in Vancouver, Canada.

One dashboard displays rotating customer quotes about the service, including comments submitted to the company or discovered on Twitter. It represents the subscriber experience in the customers' own words. Another display constantly updates Key Performance Indicators (KPIs) relevant for the service: number of customers, number of conversions created through the customers' Unbounce pages, active users, loyalty scores, and so on.

The displays use large fonts and bright colors, so they draw the eye. For everyone who works at Unbounce, the customer is present, virtually, in the workplace.

Permission Granted

If you don't have top-down commitment to manage initiatives across boundaries, you can still take action the old-fashioned way, through personal connections. If you're in marketing, make friends with customer success managers. Sit in on calls and meetings and ask them what they need. Set up a monthly check-in, or go out for coffee.

No one can keep you from having lunch together.

Remember the old saying about how it's easier to ask for forgiveness after doing something than permission before taking action? That certainly applies here. I had this discussion with a group of customer success managers at a conference run by Totango, a provider of customer success management software. One of the attendees offered his approach for gaining cooperation across multiple departments: "Sometimes it's easiest to reach across departments and not wait for top-down direction. I took it upon myself to be that person."

If enough people step up to "be that person" who reaches across boundaries, you'll end up creating a culture of value nurturing that extends beyond the marketing team.

Chapter 24

Common Challenges and Risks

In the years since the first edition of this book was published, I've interacted with many subscription-based businesses as a subscriber, spectator, fan, and occasionally adviser. Certain patterns repeat themselves in these interactions. This chapter presents common questions, challenges, objections, and problems.

As you scan through these issues, keep the following premise in mind: After the initial sign-up, your core challenges are *sustaining trust* and *nurturing value*. You can damage your business through any actions that betray customer trust or erode value.

Most often, when businesses misstep, it is because they have focused their own objectives and lost sight of customers' goals. If you sustain trust and nurture value, customers will stick around and help your business grow.

Your business is engaged in a long-term relationship with its subscribers, and everyone knows that relationships are tricky. Some people don't like change. Others are demanding. Subscription success depends on navigating the needs of those customers while also serving your own business interests.

No one said it would be easy.

Let's start with the most egregious problems: evil intentions toward your subscribers.

Tricking or Trapping Subscribers

Every now and then, I meet people who wrinkle their noses at the thought of subscription marketing, as if encountering something that smells bad.

They've experienced the unethical or lazy businesses that take advantage of their subscribers or hide behind recurring payments. These businesses live in the "dark side" of subscription marketing.

You've either heard about or experienced it yourself:

- The cable subscription that you can never cancel: the "Hotel California" business model
- The record or book club that you sign up for and get stuck with for the rest of your life
- The surprise subscription charges you find on your bill for a service that you'd signed up for but entirely forgotten about because the company went silent or you weren't using the service

Some businesses approach the subscription model with the objective of getting as much as possible from unwitting subscribers while they can. They attempt to trick, confuse, or befuddle people into paying for more than they get. In the short term, these companies often make money. In the long run, they lose trust from subscribers, and without sustained trust, a subscription business cannot thrive.

Those negative experiences make the path more difficult for every subscription business that follows.

If you want your business to stick around, commit to the idea of *sustaining value* to the customer. Return to the concept of Economic Value to the Customer (EVC), the combination of tangible and intangible value as experienced by the customer. Improving the subscriber's experience ultimately adds value to your solution and, in the long run, your business. Value is not a zero-sum game.

> In a subscription business, customer value begets business value.

The pull of the "dark side" is very strong. There may be voices, in your business or your own head, whispering temptation. Resist!

How do you know if you are trending to the dark side? Pay attention if your business model or revenue projections depend on customers making poor decisions, against their own best interests. For example:

- You count on subscribers forgetting that they've signed up, so you're careful not to interact with them around renewal time in case they don't really want to renew.

- You base revenue assumptions on the fact that people will subscribe for a higher level of service than they actually use.

- You force people into an ongoing subscription when they need a one-time service, and count on the fact that they will delay the cancellation out of neglect or inertia.

- You make subscription and renewal automatic, but cancellation is a difficult, time-consuming effort rife with pushback and arm-twisting.

It's important to spot when this thinking infects your strategy. If *you* detect it, your customers certainly will.

Potential customers and current subscribers have seen other businesses that try to trick or trap customers. They will compare your practices to those past experiences, looking for signs of malicious intentions. Earning and sustaining their trust will be more difficult.

Assuming that your business model is based on building and delivering value, let's move on to missteps or challenges in execution. From the suspicious subscriber's perspective, even the most innocent of slip-ups can look like you're switching to the dark side.

Letting Organizational Silos Fracture the Relationship

If I had to pick the single root cause of most subscription execution problems, it would be the presence of organizational silos and barriers.

From within the business, these issues are often difficult to detect. Marketing teams cannot see subscriber interactions with customer success teams, for example. Or a promise made in the marketing cycle does not filter through to those doing fulfillment.

These disconnects can result in service interruptions or glitches: Subscribers have to repeat themselves or chase problems through accounting and support teams. Severe instances of these issues appear in trouble tickets or complaints.

But the smaller hiccups are harder to detect, such as a shifting approach and messaging when interacting with the subscriber. For example, a hip, fun, "we care about you" marketing message is followed by a difficult, bureaucratic onboarding or fulfillment process. Or, a subscriber in the midst of a serious support problem receives a cheery upsell message.

The customers see these problems, but you may not.

These disconnects and glitches multiply when the marketing organization checks out once someone subscribes. Your business may have multiple, isolated groups talking to customers, with no one tracking the overall experience of the subscriber.

Successful subscription marketers collaborate consistently with those outside their own teams.

Using Customer Data Carelessly

The data you collect from customers is a terrific source for value nurturing. You can deliver usage data to individual customers, or aggregate data and share it with the world at large.

But remember: Your so-called big data is actually an enormous collection of personal information. Individual behaviors generate that data. Be careful about letting slip any details that violate subscriber privacy.

Customer data dangers include:

- Lax security that lets customer data out into the wild—data breaches
- Inappropriate sharing of individual subscriber information. If you are not diligent enough about making the data anonymous, you can let slip data that can be traced to specific individuals. If the data includes financial information that is fodder for identity theft, be extra careful, because hackers can cross-reference their way to actual identities.

In general, avoid anything that prompts a customer to wonder: *How do they know that about me?* Retargeting ads once fell into this category, but we're all becoming immune to them now. Still, think carefully before sharing subscriber data with partners, and follow local government regulations about using and sharing data.

Before you use subscriber data for anything beyond directly serving or adding value to subscribers, examine your motives. Are you doing it for your corporate fame and glory, or for the subscriber's benefit?

If the worst should happen (like a data breach) despite your best intentions, don't try to cover it up. Act quickly to regain trust by owning and fixing the problem.

Chasing Growth at All Costs: the Start-up Affliction

As a subscription house-cleaning service, Homejoy was one of the faster-growing businesses launched from Silicon Valley's near-mythical Y Combinator incubator.

After its initial service offering in 2012, the company expanded rapidly by offering low introductory rates to entice customers and fuel rapid growth. According to the research outfit Crunchbase, Homejoy raised more than $60 million between March and December 2013.

In July 2014, Homejoy shut down, a sudden demise after a meteoric rise in the otherwise stodgy home-cleaning services industry.

At the time it closed, the company was dogged by lawsuits from the independent contractors who delivered the service. But in an article in *Forbes*, Ellen Huet reported conversations with former employees who suggested that the larger problem was one of retention.

According to anonymous employees, few of the customers who signed up for the promotional rates stuck around; retention rates were horrific. In chasing growth, the company ignored, or even damaged, its retention.

It's the curse of the well-funded start-up that tries to prove itself to investors. In chasing growth, start-ups often neglect retention.

One founder starting a subscription box company stated his situation this way: "The idea of nurturing the customer is great. But I really need to focus on acquiring new customers right now. I'll think about value nurturing later."

For a start-up that doesn't focus on its subscribers, that elusive "later" may never arrive.

Every start-up must face two key realities about growth and retention:

1. You will never feel like you have "enough" new leads or customers. As you grow, you reset the bar for what "enough" looks like.

2. Retention is essential to growth. For every subscriber who leaves, you must find a replacement to stay even before you can start growing. Plus, those satisfied customers are your best source of leads and referrals—a growth engine.

The start-up growth affliction is not inevitable. Enterprise messaging and collaboration provider Slack began at about the same time that Homejoy shut down: summer 2013. It reached a billion dollars in valuation in record time. Its success was built, in part, on the fact that the company focused on providing value to its customers from day one. Slack's users became the Slack sales and marketing force.

If you're interested in growth-hacking strategies, take a long, hard look at the value you provide to subscribers, no matter how small you are. The best time to build value nurturing into the culture is at the outset.

Removing Value from Subscribers

Any psychologist or behavioral economist will tell you that human beings are loss averse. We simply do not like giving up something that we already have, and will take extra actions to avoid losses. Subscription businesses must remember this fact about their customers.

As your business grows and evolves, you will adapt. Whenever possible, avoid making changes that customer might perceive as losses.

For example, some companies launch with a freemium model: free service for most people, premium for others. But they have no plan to scale up. The free service users love it and spread the word, leading to rapid growth. Hampered by their own success, the company strips functionality from the free version, assuming that all those happy users will gladly upgrade to a paid version. After all, they've been getting those features without paying so far, right?

Rather than being grateful for the months or years of free use, those formerly happy subscribers feel betrayed and cheated. Many will not upgrade for that reason. A few complain loudly on social media about corporate greed.

You might run into a similar problem when trying to change pricing models. Netflix encounters friction every time it raises prices.

I blame loss aversion, or our human tendency to fear losses more than we value gains. It doesn't take long for people to feel entitled to something that they've been given for free. When that thing is taken from us, we feel cheated. The pain of the loss colors our judgment.

The morals of this story are:

1. If you choose a freemium model, make sure it's one that you can sustain through growth.

2. If you have to change a pricing model or service, try to avoid framing it as a loss. For example, if you raise prices, can you add features at the same time? Is there any way to present the situation as a potential gain rather than a certain loss?

Death by Pricing Complexity

Pricing is one of the trickiest parts of a subscription business.

- The price must sustain the business, offsetting the cost of customer acquisition as well as covering ongoing service delivery and leaving room for profit.

- The price should reflect the customer expectations for the value delivered from the service (the Economic Value to the Customer)

- Pricing levels also serve to *set* customer expectations and determine which customers you attract.

Setting your price too low can not only land you in trouble financially, but can also attract the bargain-hunter customers who may not renew or who are always shopping for a better deal. Find the price point that attracts those customers who value what you offer and are likely to remain long-term, loyal subscribers.

In addition to the actual pricing numbers, determine how complex your pricing plan should be. How many tiers or options should you offer?

People like choices. In today's business environment, we want and expect some degree of choice in the things we buy. Having choices gives us a sense of control, and having control makes us happy.

But more is not better when it comes to choices. When presented with a large number of options, we have to engage our rational, analytical minds and expend energy figuring out the best option. If you're selling complex enterprise software, for example, that analysis may be part of the sales cycle. But in general, you can accelerate sales cycles by *minimizing* the cognitive effort involved in making a decision.

Here's the interesting part: Cognitive science tells us that having *too many* choices often leads to regret. After we make the difficult decision, we are more likely to regret the choice we made. We might rethink it, or wonder whether one of the other options was better.

Giving potential customers too many choices is a recipe for creating unhappy customers.

Look at your own experiences for guidance. For example, the Netflix streaming video service offers three options: basic, standard, and premium. A full-page chart explains the differences, which really come down to high-definition formats and the number of concurrent screens. It shouldn't take a potential subscriber long to make that decision.

What if your solution is inherently more complex? Consider breaking down the decision process into steps with a few options at each phase. Take a look at Adobe Creative Cloud, which lets you subscribe to bundled or individual applications. The company guides you through the options in a series of easier questions:

- Do you want a bundle or a single app?
- If a single app, which one?

Let prospective subscribers guide themselves, minimizing the cognitive load of deciding and the potential for regret when they are done.

Neglecting a Declining Subscription Base

This last execution issue is for those businesses that have long been in a subscription model, but find that their subscription base is shrinking.

The Subscription Economy is disrupting many businesses that already use subscriptions like consumer media (newspapers, magazines). What do you do if you have a mature subscription base that has stopped growing? Even if loyal subscribers aren't churning, if you are not able to attract many new ones, the overall base declines through natural attrition.

Consider expanding your target market by adding or shifting subscription offerings. That loyal customer base is a significant asset that can help you make the change, if you think creatively about what you're doing.

National Public Radio would seem to be an archaic model: publicly funded radio offered over the air. In addition to government support, NPR stations draw support from listeners, who "subscribe" with their donations.

NPR has remained fresh and relevant by constantly looking beyond its origins. It jumped quickly into the podcasting trend, with great success. To further serve and expand its listeners, the organization offers the NPR One mobile app. This app lets listeners create customized streams of audio content, including both national and local news, and NPR podcasts alongside podcasts from other sources. Usage of the app is growing steadily.

The venerable *New Yorker* magazine has been a fixture in my life since I was a child, thumbing through my parents' weekly issues to find cartoons that I could understand. That magazine is spreading its reach to social media and the online world, finding new ways to deliver value to existing (and new) subscribers. For example, an iPhone app lets you listen to featured poets reading the works published in the print magazine.

Start with the value that you offer subscribers, and find ways to extend it.

Chapter 25

Four Fundamental Rules of Value Nurturing

To support and nurture customers after the sale, abide by a few basic rules:

1. Value starts with the customer
2. Be human, but consistent
3. Handle mistakes with grace
4. Don't be creepy

These guidelines aren't unique to value nurturing. You probably practice most or all of them today, and we've already covered them in other parts of this book. But with a subscription model, in which you maintain an ongoing relationship with the customer, these rules are not optional. Let's revisit them.

Rule #1: Value Starts with the Customer

Run a quick litmus test on every value-nurturing campaign: Is it about your business or the customer?

To find long-term success, your business must meet your *customers'* needs. A clever video that wins awards and goes viral is meaningless from a value-nurturing perspective unless your customers find it entertaining or useful.

> Value nurturing begins with the customer's perspective.

Particularly in business-to-business industries, marketing organizations spend a great deal of time and money communicating the wondrous features of their solutions. Some technology enthusiasts cannot differentiate between a product feature and its benefit to the customer.

Big brands are accustomed to being the heroes of their own stories. I've heard this request: "We need an article about how visionary our CEO is—let's make it all about him." Sometimes you have to cater to stakeholders other than the customer. But don't confuse this with creating content that customers can use.

Value nurturing puts the customer at the center of the story.

In the book *Winning the Story Wars*, Jonah Sachs writes about the long history of "inadequacy marketing," or marketing based on the idea that prospects *lack* something that can only be fixed with a purchase. He writes:

> Inadequacy stories encourage immature emotions like greed, vanity, and insecurity by telling us that we are somehow incomplete. These stories then offer to remove the discomfort of those emotions with a simple purchase or association with a brand.

With inadequacy marketing, the hero of every story is the product, service, or the brand providing it. We are surrounded by messages that we can be smarter, richer, cooler, or less thirsty if we simply buy the right products.

Sachs contrasts this approach with what he calls "empowerment marketing," or marketing in a way that helps customers on their own paths to growth or maturity. When you practice empowerment marketing, the customer is the hero of your stories. Your solution fills one of many possible roles in the customer's journey, supporting and enabling the customer.

Consider Apple's advertisements that show people doing wonderful or creative things with the iPad. The device is the enabler, while the Apple *customers* are the stars.

Once someone becomes a subscription customer, inadequacy marketing ceases to be effective. If your solution doesn't address a genuine need rather than a manufactured inadequacy, the customer will catch on and stop subscribing. If you rely on empowerment marketing, then your messages continue to resonate with people, urging them to step up into the leading role.

Value nurturing is all about joining and supporting the subscribers on their journeys. If your solution empowers customers, then your business will also succeed.

Rule #2: Be Human, But Consistent

We expect a lot from the organizations we do business with.

On one hand, we understand that every business is a collection of people. As customers, we want to interact with real people when we have a problem or question. Employees may blog or tweet in their own names, and company "About Us" web pages show photos and profile employees to humanize the business.

On the other hand, we expect consistency across all parts of a business. Whether in a sales or service interaction, we don't want to repeat ourselves, or get mixed messages. In this sense, we see businesses as single entities.

Our expectations for both consistency and humanity have implications for marketing in the Subscription Economy. Marketing messages, tone, and style create expectations for interactions beyond the sale. Marketing defines the personality for the overall brand, and the rest of the business must live up to it.

Whatever personality you express, it should be consistent with your business and the people in it. If you cast your business as a caring, values-driven organization, then you must behave in that manner when interacting with customers in all parts of the business.

One way to ensure consistency is to create a brand style guide and share it throughout the company, *beyond* the marketing organization.

Tone and style extend beyond your written communications to online interactions, phone conversations, and website pages. For example, if you click a broken link on the IBM website, you receive a polite and helpful error page, headlined "Our apologies..." that includes links for suggested actions and assistance. It's a great fit for a company that wants to be a trusted business and technology adviser.

In contrast, the Geek Squad is a technical support business built on a sense of fun. Its tagline is "Serving the Public, Policing Technology and Protecting the World." Employees carry "Special Agent" badges and drive GeekMobile® vehicles to customer sites.

If you reach the error page on the GeekSquad website, you'll find a page with the headline "OMG! YOU BROKE THE INTERWEBS!" The message continues: "Quick! Click one of the working links before the fabric of space and time begins to unravel. Oh, and sorry for the inconvenience."

In each case, the expression of the brand personality flows all the way to the error page.

That brings us to the essential corollary to this rule. If "to err is human," then you'd better know how to handle mistakes well.

Rule #3: Handle Your Mistakes with Grace

In business as in life, when you make a mistake, own up to it and make it right.

When you engage honestly with your customers, you get negative feedback that isn't fun to hear. It's a golden opportunity. For every customer with a genuine problem, assume that dozens of others feel the same pain but say nothing. By finding and addressing the pain points, you can make things better for many others. Be grateful to complaining customers, because they're giving you the insight to improve.

When you hear about a problem or make a mistake, it's best to deal with it quickly and openly. Social media channels magnify any mistakes, but if you deal with them openly, they disappear eventually. Try to cover up or blame the customer, however, and you'll reach a new level of negative exposure.

In today's highly transparent world, nothing makes your brand look worse than picking a fight with a customer.

One historic hotel in New York City fined its wedding customers $500 if anyone involved with the wedding wrote a negative online review. That's a terrible idea for oh-so-many reasons, and it blew up on social media. (Moral of the story for consumers: if you're booking a wedding venue, read the contract before you sign.)

Rule #4: Don't Be Creepy

When it comes to engaging with current customers, look for the line dividing personalized from "Big Brother" and creepy. Don't cross that line.

Technology and big data deliver real-time insight into customers' online behavior. You can use this insight to create highly targeted campaigns that delight customers. But if you stalk your customers online and interrupt them with messages that demonstrate that you're watching their behavior, some people will feel spooked.

What delights one person might distress another. Understand your customers. Where possible, offer people a chance to opt out if they find a campaign intrusive. This is particularly the case if someone visits your website and believes they are anonymous (they haven't logged on). Be careful about what you communicate unless you've explicitly asked permission to install a cookie or leave them logged on. No one wants to do business with Big Brother.

If you're not sure whether a campaign or idea goes too far, test it with several customers and see if you're hitting their creep factor. What matters is what *they* think, not what you think. As an added bonus, asking for advice is a technique for nurturing value. You may strengthen the customer relationship because you asked.

Chapter 26

The Marketing Opportunity

The strategies in this book are based on a central truth: Subscription-based businesses maintain ongoing relationships with their customers far beyond the initial sign-up. Customer marketing isn't a "nice-to-have" function—it's essential.

For marketers, the challenges of adapting to the subscription trend are many. But I'd argue that there's never been a better time to be in marketing if you want a chance to make a difference in your business. As a marketing professional, you have license be creative. You can expand your reach, creating value for your business and its customers.

Creativity Needed

The old rules of marketing don't apply; you hereby have permission to make up new ones. When it comes to marketing for subscriptions, everyone is learning on the job, and nobody has all the answers—even the marketing gurus.

Huge budgets are nice but not necessary. Marketing powerhouses like Coca-Cola and Procter & Gamble face genuine challenges from smaller businesses that understand their markets intimately. Content marketing, social media, and digital marketing level the playing field. Changing business models are creating new platforms for delivering value.

With storytelling as a marketing imperative, creativity is at a premium. As the examples in Part Two illustrate, people who look beyond the usual ways of doing things can make a huge impact with their customers.

Remember, you are participating in a constantly evolving lesson in subscription marketing: Look around and learn.

Filling Bigger Shoes

You may find yourself working outside your comfort zone as an advocate for customer value. Step into that challenge. A subscription business model presents marketers with the opportunity to play a larger role, reaching beyond traditional pre-sales activities and influencing the business direction and revenues directly. If that's going to happen, you have learn to collaborate closely with all parts of the business involved in maintaining the customer relationship.

Many of the examples in this book extend beyond the marketing organization. The usual suspects involved in customer success include customer support and renewal sales or account management teams. You may also work with product designers, training and documentation, operations staff, and others to set and execute on customer expectations.

The broader your reach within your organization, the larger your potential impact on the subscriber's experience.

Increasing Business Value

Marketing is no longer just about getting to the sale. To keep subscription customers renewing and reengaging, you have to provide real value and solve problems. Doing so requires a deep understanding of the customer.

A growing number of people want to know the *values* of the organizations that they do business with. The need to strengthen ongoing relationships with customers makes it critical for businesses to understand and claim their *own* values. The good news is that employees of value-driven companies are more engaged at work.

You just might have more fun.

Changing the World

I'll end this book with my optimistic vision of how the Subscription Economy can make the world a better place.

Let's start with this premise: Successful subscription businesses adopt a long-term perspective toward customer relationships. Thus, the subscription business model weakens the short-term profit focus that drives our current financial system. That's a good thing, because short-term profit motivation can create sustained damage. (Witness environmental damages or the economic crisis of 2008.)

Customer loyalty is critical for subscription success. Those businesses that align with their customers' deeper values are going to have a significant advantage. We should start to see more values-driven organizations. Businesses that take an ethical or values-based stance can score a competitive advantage.

Think about the impact of that equation at scale across society. The world economy is incredibly powerful. If it slowly redirects its efforts to the issues people care about, the potential impact is enormous. And that, my friends, is how the Subscription Economy can change the world.

Acknowledgments

I owe thanks to every client I have worked with, each sub-scriber to the Subscription Marketing list, and each reader or listener who has reached out with their thoughts and stories. But if I were to name them all, the list of people would be at least as long as the book itself. So, recognize that what follows is merely the tip of my gratitude iceberg.

For this second edition, I owe a particular debt of thanks to the people on my Subscription Marketing email list and the readers of the first edition. Time and again, people have contacted me with stories, suggestions, and insights that have made this book better.

Others have graciously let me share their stories and opinions in this edition. Irit Eizips and Lincoln Murphy have both provided invaluable guidance into customer success. Sarah E. Brown offered insight into her Voice of the Customer research. Rollis Fontenot III spent time patiently explaining the recruiting business to me. Ryan Engeley has shared the Unbounce story with me on multiple occasions. Will Sullivan graciously contributed the story of The Right Margin's WriterHangout team on Slack. Ranan Lachman has delighted me with stories from Pley.com more than once.

Roger C. Parker belongs in a category of his own in this regard; he has been remarkably supportive for a couple of years, providing feedback, coming up with interesting subscription businesses, and always having a great idea to share.

Thanks to Carolyn Hotchkiss for telling me about Babson's Define campaign, and to Sarah Sykora for sharing detailed information about the school's objectives and results from the campaign.

Others who have provided invaluable contributions to spreading the word about subscription marketing include Douglas Burdett (of the wonderful Marketing Book podcast), Tom Krakeler and Rachel English of Zuora, Shira Abel, Bill Cushard of ServiceRocket, and Samantha Stone of the marketing Advisory Network.

The draft has also benefitted from the feedback of early readers, including Michelle Langford of the Subscription Trade Association. Particular thanks go to Jennifer Havice, Earl Greene, and Brian Mullin for stepping forward and sharing their stories and expertise.

When it comes to gathering the detailed content for the examples and illustrations, I owe thanks to many sources. Amy Konary at IDC has helped me track down sources for their research for both editions of the book. Gabe Weisert has given me access to Zuora's research and analysis of the Subscription Economy, and Return Path's Daniel Incandela let me borrow their koala. MarketingProfs, Cone Communications, The CMO Survey, Edelman Research, Adobe, and Totango have given me access to research that enriches the content.

At ServiceSource, particular thanks go to Randy Brasche, Jim Dunham, and everyone who has shared with me their expertise on recurring revenues. They helped to set me on this path.

This book as it appears before you has benefitted from the efforts and advice of many individuals. I'm grateful for Holly Brady's guidance and Thomas McGee's brilliant cover design. Laurie Gibson and Mark Rhynsburger have improved the text with their editorial acumen.

Ongoing encouragement, support, and feedback have been welcome from many people, including Lisa Abbott, Christopher Bartik, Kaiser Mulla-Feroze, Tracey Sestilli, John Morgan, John Robb, Tom Hogan, Carol Broadbent, Stephan Hovnanian ... the list never ends. How lucky am I?

I have relied heavily on inspiration (and quotes) from many authors I admire. Early and ongoing support from David Meerman Scott, Ann Handley, and Joe Pulizzi provided essential wind in my sails at the start of this journey. I continue to be inspired by Kathy Klotz Guest, Robbie Kellman Baxter, and Linda Popky, as well as Jonah Sachs, Tyler Montague, and Simon Mainwaring.

Closer to home, my family has been endlessly patient and supportive through the publication of this book—twice! They have brought me examples of subscription successes, found errors, and provided suggestions to make the book better. I am forever grateful for their love and support.

Resources and Notes

Recommended Reading

If you're looking for books to consult as you implement the strategies discussed in this book, here are a few good companions.

The Automatic Customer by John Warrillow (Portfolio). This book identifies and labels *nine* distinct variations on the business model. Warrillow discusses the differences in these variations, as well as their fit for various industries and businesses.

Brand Against the Machine, by John Morgan (Wiley). This book is a compelling discussion of the realities of branding in today's world. It's full of actionable insight, and aligns well with value-nurturing objectives of building a customer-focused brand and earning customer trust.

Branding Basics for Small Businesses, by Maria Ross (NorLights Press). I read the book after hearing Ross talk. Despite the title, her no-nonsense approach to branding makes sense for businesses of all sizes. She offers great advice about true brand consistency.

Content. Inc.: How Entrepreneurs Use Content to Build Massive Audiences and Create Radically Successful Businesses, by Joe Pulizzi (McGraw-Hill Education). Pulizzi proposes that we begin with subscription content, and then build out to figure out what they should sell. A company founded on this premise will develop a corporate culture based on adding value through content and aligning with customers' values—both core value-nurturing practices.

The Difference: The One Page Method for Reimagining Your Business and Reinventing Your Marketing, by Bernadette Jiwa (The Story Of Telling Press). This book is a fast but inspiring read, calling us to create a real difference in customers' lives.

Epic Content Marketing, by Joe Pulizzi (McGraw-Hill Education). Pulizzi compiles everything you might need to know about content marketing in one place. It's the modern content marketer's definitive source.

Everybody Writes: Your Go-To Guide for Creating Ridiculously Good Content, by Ann Handley (Wiley). I love Ann Handley's writing—here's your chance to find out why it's so good. This book offers insight into how to make marketing writing both fun and personable. Even if you're an expert writer, you'll find much to love in this book.

Marketing Above the Noise, by Linda Popky (Bibliomotion). This book is a comprehensive tour of effective marketing practices, incorporating the latest trends but not letting them distract the reader from long-term objectives. Popky also touches on the topic of marketing to customers: "Your marketing should reinforce the wisdom of the customer's choice."

The Membership Economy, by Robbie Kellman Baxter (McGraw-Hill Education). In *The Membership Economy,* Baxter shares her insider's perspective into the challenges and opportunities of building a membership-based business. After the necessary discussion of terminology and trends, she dives into seven key strategies and tactics for membership businesses, including onboarding, pricing, and technology.

The New Rules of Sales and Service, by David Meerman Scott (Wiley). David Meerman Scott redefined marketing several years ago, with his *New Rules of Marketing and PR.* In this book, he highlights the challenges of ongoing customer engagement. The topic is highly relevant for a marketer in a subscription-based business, because the divisions between marketing, sales, and service are shrinking.

Stop Boring Me: How to Create Kick-Ass Marketing, Products and Ideas Through the Power of Improv, by Kathy Klotz-Guest (Substantium). The book offers guidance for creating better, more effective marketing content by applying the essential principles of improv comedy. As you might expect, reading it is fun; the text is filled with entertaining stories as well as spot-on examples.

Thinking Fast and Slow, by Daniel Kahneman (Farrar, Straus and Giroux). He may have won the Nobel Prize for Economics, but marketers everywhere should offer up thanks to Kahneman for explaining our irrational (and lazy) thought systems. This book reveals the vagaries of human decisions and thoughts.

To Sell Is Human, by Daniel Pink (Riverhead Books). This book is less about sales and more about human nature, empathy, and persuasion. It's an entertaining read filled with useful insight.

True Story: How to Combine Story and Action to Transform Your Business, by Ty Montague (Harvard Business Review Press). This book insists that brands must go beyond storytelling to story*doing*. Montague describes how an authentic corporate metastory transcends marketing and informs business actions.

Winning the Story Wars, by Jonah Sachs (Harvard Business Review Press). This book elevates marketing to another level, calling on Joseph Campbell's hero's journey, cultural myths, and Maslow's hierarchy of needs. Its call for an end to "inadequacy" marketing and a new, empowering approach to marketing is inspiring.

Youtility: Why Smart Marketing is about Help, Not Hype, by Jay Baer (Penguin Group LLC). The title encapsulates the meaning of the book and Baer's approach to marketing, combining utility with a focus on the customer or audience. In the subscription marketing context, the concepts also apply when you're nurturing value for existing customers. By focusing on being helpful and practicing Youtility, marketers add value outside the solutions they sell.

Notes

Want to find some of the research mentioned in the text?

Introduction: Find the full Subscription Economy Index report on the Zuora website (zuora.com).

Chapter 1: To learn more about the circular economy, visit the Ellen MacArthur Foundation site.

Chapter 3: Find the Scout Analytics/Service Source research about the time to profitability for a subscription customer in the blog post titled "Calculating Customer Lifetime Value" on the ServiceSource blog.

Chapter 8: Check out B.J Fogg's research into habit change on his website, bjfogg.com, on the Persuasive Technology website at captology.stanford.edu, or in his textbook, *Persuasive Technology*.

Chapter 11: The ThreatMetrix Cybercrime Threat Map is accessible from the Resources section of the ThreatMetrix website at www.threatmetrix.com.

Chapter 13: The data about podcasting listener growth is from Edison Research, The Infinite Dial 2016, available at EdisonResearch.com. You can also find the Edison Research Interactive Advertising Bureau study on the website.

Chapter 18: The Ben Horowitz quote about story and strategy comes from Carmine Gallo's article "Your Story Is Your Strategy, Says VC Who Backed Facebook and Twitter" on Forbes.com, April 29, 2014.

Chapter 19: Download the Cone Communications/Ebiquity Global CSR study from the Cone Communication research blog.

Chapter 21: Net Promoter, Net Promoter Score, and NPS are trademarks of Satmetrix Systems, Inc., Bain & Company, Inc., and Fred Reichheld.

Chapter 24: The article "What Really Killed Homejoy," by Ellen Huet appeared in Forbes, July 23, 2015.

About the Author

Anne Janzer is an award-winning author on a mission to help writers and marketers communicate more effectively.

As a professional writer, she has worked with more than one hundred technology companies. She offers online courses workshops on writing for marketers and others who communicate about technical topics.

Anne is author of three other books: *The Writer's Process*, *The Workplace Writer's Process*, and *Writing to Be Understood: What Works and Why*. Her books have won awards from Foreword Reviews, Reader's Favorite, and IndieReader.

She contributes to numerous industry publications and blogs, and posts regularly about writing and marketing on her website at AnneJanzer.com.

Anne lives in Mountain View, California, surrounded by self-driving cars and coding enthusiasts. Still, nothing makes her quite as happy as a good book.

Connect on Social Media

Website: AnneJanzer.com

Twitter: @AnneJanzer

Facebook: Anne H Janzer

LinkedIn: Anne H Janzer

Join the Subscription Marketing Group

Are you interested in joining an ongoing discussion about subscription marketing? Sign up for the Subscription Marketing group from AnneJanzer.com. You'll receive new resources and examples. And I'd love to hear what you think.

Share Your Thoughts

If you liked the strategies in this book, leave a review (on Amazon, Goodreads, or wherever you may have found the book). Spread the word.

Index

AAA, 94
Adagio Teas, 32, 109-110
Adobe, 31-32, 25, 95, 99
  CMO.com, 95
  Creative Cloud, 31, 35, 185
  Marketing Cloud, 31, 95
  revenues, 32
advocacy marketing, 83, 107-113, 185
advocates, 54, 80, 82, 107-113, 138, 166
Amazon, 1, 19, 20, 33, 91, 109
  Anticipatory shipping, 20
  CreateSpace, 91
  Prime, 19, 33
  Subscribe and Save store, 19
American Express OPEN Forum, 104
Apple, 65, 80, 191
Ariely, Dan, 111
Ascend HR Corp., 20, 36-38
The Automatic Customer (Warrillow), 28, 205
average revenue per account, 41, 145, 150
B2B, 9, 40, 50, 109, 165
B corporations, 133-134
benefit corporations, 133-134
Babson College, 115-117
Baer, Jay, 94, 208
Baxter, Robbie Kellman, 16, 27-28, 203, 206
Birchbox, 95
Blizzard Entertainment, 121-122
brand recognition, 48, 49, 96
Brown, Sarah E., 171, 201
Buffer, 67

Butterfield, Stewart, 71
celebration, 89-91, 167
churn, 4-7, 29, 35, 42, 43, 145-152, 160, 186
cloud software, 2, 17, 18, 30, 31
CMO.com, 95
Content Inc. (Pulizzi), 33-34
Content Marketing Institute, 33
Cratejoy, 23
CreateSpace, 91
Creative Cloud, 31, 35, 185
customer
  journey, 8, 50 52, 65, 166
  launch plan, 63-68, 158
  lifetime value, 40, 56, 146, 150, 152
  loyalty, 7, 9, 59, 77, 86, 94, 109-112, 141, 148-149, 160, 168, 179, 199
  onboarding, 29, 64, 67, 68, 72, 136, 166, 170, 179
  milestones, 72, 90, 166
  retention, 6, 51, 55-56, 145-148, 150, 152, 159, 160, 169, 171, 181-182
  stories, 81-83, 155, 161
customer success, 8, 9, 30, 34,44, 52, 71, 72, 137, 164-168, 201
  CSM, 54, 58, 164-167, 169, 170
  dashboards, 171-172
  marketing and, 44, 108, 136, 172, 198
  teams, 8, 9, 34, 136, 137, 161, 163-168
data, 24, 58, 77, 85-87, 97-98, 166, 179-180

aggregated, 86-87
big data, 129, 180, 194
leaks, 180
usage, 85-86, 90, 97
Dickens, Charles, 15
Dollar Shave Club, 98
economic value to customer
(EVC), 56, 79, 177
Edison Research, 96, 209
Eizips, Irit, 165-167, 201
Engeley, Ryan, 171-172, 201
Facebook, 102, 103, 127, 157
First & Fastest, 94-95
Fitbit, 24, 90
Fogg, B.J., 75, 209
Fontenot, Rollis, 36-37, 201
free trial, 5, 9, 59, 135-141
freemium, 24, 138-139, 183
French Laundry, 69-70
gamification
Gartner Hype Cycle
Gascoigne, Joel, 67
Geek Squad, 193
Guest, Kathy Klotz, 99, 203,
207
Haiku Deck, 66
habit formation, 75-77
Happy Money (Dunn and Nor-
ton), 57
Headspace, 76
Hootsuite, 112-113
Hulick, Samuel, 68
IDC, 18, 202
Internet of Things (IOT), 23-24
Kaushik, Avinash, 47
Keller, Thomas, 69-70
Lachman, Ranan, 201
lead generation, 41, 44, 45, 49,
53-55, 116, 152, 159, 166
lead nurturing, 48, 54, 55, 59,
116, 137
loss aversion, 183
Lyft, 23, 86, 97

magazines, 2, 15, 82, 93-95, 105,
186, 187
Mainwaring, Simon, 117, 133,
203
marketing
advocacy, 83, 107-113, 185
automation, 45, 156, 158, 166
and sales, 6, 40, 44-45, 48,
136-137, 164- 168, 170
content marketing, 93, 96,
156-157, 198, 206
email, 90, 158, 166
funnels, 9, 47-51
metrics, 45, 56, 145-146, 150,
152, 159-160, 169
relevance, 39-40
social media, 101-103, 156-
157
The Membership Economy (Baxter),
16, 27-28, 208
Microsoft, 1, 18, 72
milestones, 72, 90, 166
Misbehaving (Thaler), 64
Montague, Ty, 123, 203, 208
Murphy, Lincoln, 72, 201
National Public Radio (NPR),
186
Net Promoter Score, 145, 149,
209
New Rules of Sales and Service
(Scott), 45, 93, 207
newspapers, 2, 15, 186
onboarding, 29, 64, 67, 68, 72,
136, 166, 170, 179
pain of paying, 32
Parker, Roger C., 95, 202
Patagonia, 126, 134
Pley.com, 117-118, 201
podcasts, 80, 96-97, 124, 171,
186-187, 209
Predictably Irrational (Ariely), 111
Pulizzi, Joe, 33, 157, 203
Rainmaker, 140
Red Bull, 105

retention, customer, 6, 51, 55-56, 145-148, 150, 152, 159, 160, 169, 171, 181-182
Return Path, 119-120, 202
revenue growth, 18, 35, 45, 56, 57, 146-148, 159
The Right Margin, 102-103, 201
Salesforce, 17, 104, 113
sales compensation, 153, 169
SAP, 124-125
Scott, David Meerman, 45, 93, 203, 207
ServiceRocket, 171, 202
ServiceSource, 42, 64, 203, 208
Sharing Economy, 23, 117
Shore Line Interurban Historical Society, 94
Slack, 71, 102-103, 157, 182
social media, 67, 83, 93, 101-103, 109, 111, 128, 156-157, 193-194
software-as-a-service (SaaS), 17
start-ups, 3, 9, 22, 23, 27-28, 33-34, 89, 102, 133, 148, 152, 167, 181-2
Stop Boring Me! (Guest), 99, 207
subscriptions
  as marketing, 32-33
  communities, 3, 16, 83, 94, 101-105, 117-118, 157
  models, 3, 8, 9, 15-25, 27-28, 36-38, 40, 45, 49, 57, 176, 189
  pricing, 30, 35-37, 40, 183-184
  trial, 28-30, 135-141
subscription boxes, 2, 15, 22-23, 95, 117, 181

Subscription Economy, 3-6, 15, 17, 25, 28, 39, 45, 56, 186, 192, 199-200
Subscription Economy Index, 3-5, 208
Sustainability, 124-125
Sullivan, Will, 103, 201
Sykora, Sarah, 116, 202
Thaler, Richard, 64
ThreatMetrix, 87, 209
Toms Shoes, 131-132
triple bottom line, 133
Tzuo, Tien, 25
Unbounce, 171-172, 201
Unilever, 3, 125-126, 134
value nurturing, 7, 9-10, 51, 53-59, 81, 107, 117, 137, 141, 145-153, 155, 157, 159-160, 170, 171, 189-191
values-based marketing, 125-126, 128-129, 200
video, 22, 65, 70, 80, 93, 95, 98, 99, 124, 128, 132, 137, 140, 157, 159
Warrillow, John, 28, 205
Waze, 77
We First (Mainwaring), 117, 133
Webinars, 80, 140, 161, 167, 171
welcome email, 66-67, 102
Winston, Andrew, 128-129
WriterHangout, 102-103, 201
Youtility (Baer), 94, 208
Zendesk, 83
Zipcar, 23, 71
Zuora, 3-5, 25, 202, 208
Zvenyach, V. David, 129

Made in the USA
Lexington, KY
24 June 2019